A Guide to the Film BULLY:

Fostering Empathy and Action in Schools

Created to accompany the film BULLY,
directed by Lee Hirsch

FACING
HISTORY
AND
OURSELVES

A Facing History and Ourselves Guide

Facing History and Ourselves is an international educational and professional development organization whose mission is to engage students of diverse backgrounds in an examination of racism, prejudice, and antisemitism in order to promote the development of a more humane and informed citizenry. By studying the historical development of the Holocaust and other examples of genocide, students make the essential connection between history and the moral choices they confront in their own lives. For more information about Facing History and Ourselves, please visit our website at *www.facinghistory.org*.

Cover art credit and credits for photos on pages 12, 13, and 14: Lee Hirsch/The Weinstein Company

To download a PDF of this guide free of charge, please visit *www.facinghistory.org/safeschools*.

ISBN-13: 978-0-9837870-4-4
ISBN-10: 0983787042

Facing History and Ourselves Headquarters
16 Hurd Road
Brookline, MA 02445-6919

FACING
HISTORY
AND
OURSELVES

About Facing History and Ourselves

Facing History and Ourselves is a nonprofit educational organization whose mission is to engage students of diverse backgrounds in an examination of racism, prejudice, and antisemitism in order to promote a more humane and informed citizenry. As the name Facing History and Ourselves implies, the organization helps teachers and their students make the essential connections between history and the moral choices they confront in their own lives, and offers a framework and a vocabulary for analyzing the meaning and responsibility of citizenship and the tools to recognize bigotry and indifference in their own worlds. Through a rigorous examination of the failure of democracy in Germany during the 1920s and '30s and the steps leading to the Holocaust, along with other examples of hatred, collective violence, and genocide in the past century, Facing History and Ourselves provides educators with tools for teaching history and ethics, and for helping their students learn to combat prejudice with compassion, indifference with participation, myth and misinformation with knowledge.

Believing that no classroom exists in isolation, Facing History and Ourselves offers programs and materials to a broad audience of students, parents, teachers, civic leaders, and all of those who play a role in the education of young people. Through significant higher education partnerships, Facing History and Ourselves also reaches and impacts teachers before they enter their classrooms.

By studying the choices that led to critical episodes in history, students learn how issues of identity and membership, ethics and judgment have meaning today and in the future. Facing History and Ourselves' resource books provide a meticulously researched yet flexible structure for examining complex events and ideas. Educators can select appropriate readings and draw on additional resources available online or from our comprehensive lending library.

Our foundational resource book, *Facing History and Ourselves: Holocaust and Human Behavior,* embodies a sequence of study that begins with identity—first individual identity and then group and national identities, with their definitions of membership. From there the program examines the failure of democracy in Germany and the steps leading to the Holocaust—the most documented case of twentieth-century indifference, de-humanization, hatred, racism, antisemitism, and mass murder. It goes on to explore difficult questions of judgment, memory, and legacy, and the necessity for responsible participation to prevent injustice. Facing History and Ourselves then returns to the theme of civic participation to examine stories of individuals, groups, and nations who have worked to build just and inclusive communities and whose stories illuminate the courage, compassion, and political will that are needed to protect democracy today and in generations to come. Other examples in which civic dilemmas test democracy, such as the Armenian Genocide and the US civil rights movement, expand and deepen the connection between history and the choices we face today and in the future.

Facing History and Ourselves has offices or resource centers in the United States, Canada, and the United Kingdom, as well as in-depth partnerships in Rwanda, South Africa, and Northern Ireland. Facing History and Ourselves' outreach is global, with educators trained in more than 80 countries and delivery of our resources through a website accessed worldwide with online content delivery, a program for international fellows, and a set of NGO partnerships. By convening conferences of scholars, theologians, educators, and journalists, Facing History and Ourselves' materials are kept timely, relevant, and responsive to salient issues of global citizenship in the twenty-first century.

For more than 30 years, Facing History and Ourselves has challenged students and educators to connect the complexities of the past to the moral and ethical issues of today. They explore democratic values and consider what it means to exercise one's rights and responsibilities in the service of a more humane and compassionate world. They become aware that "little things are big"—seemingly minor decisions can have a major impact and change the course of history.

For more about Facing History and Ourselves, visit our website at *www.facinghistory.org.*

About BULLY

This year, more than 13 million American kids will be bullied, making it the most common form of violence young people in the US experience. Directed by Sundance and Emmy Award-winning filmmaker Lee Hirsch, BULLY is a beautifully cinematic, character-driven documentary—at its heart are those with the most at stake and whose stories each represent a different facet of this bullying crisis.

Following five kids and families over the course of a school year, the film confronts bullying's most tragic outcomes, including the stories of two families who've lost children to suicide and a mother who waits to learn the fate of her 14-year-old daughter, incarcerated after bringing a gun on her school bus. With rare access to the Sioux City Community School District, the film also gives an intimate glimpse into school buses, classrooms, cafeterias, and even principals' offices, offering insight into the often cruel world of children, as teachers, administrators, and parents struggle to find answers.

While the stories examine the dire consequences of bullying, they also give testimony to the courage and strength of the victims of bullying and seek to inspire real changes in the way we deal with bullying as parents, teachers, children, and in society as a whole. Through the power of these stories, BULLY aims to be a catalyst for change and to turn the tide on an epidemic of violence that has touched every community in the United States—and far beyond.

Film Credits

BULLY, a film by Lee Hirsch
Presented by Where We Live Films
in association with BeCause Foundation
The Einhorn Family Charitable Trust
The Waitt Institute for Violence Prevention

Directed by Lee Hirsch
Executive Producer Cindy Waitt

ON THE WEB

For more information about BULLY, visit the website of The Bully Project Social Action Campaign at *www.thebullyproject.com*

Acknowledgments

Primary Writer: Daniel Sigward

Facing History and Ourselves extends special recognition to Lee Hirsch, director of BULLY, for shining a spotlight on the issue of bullying in schools through his film and collaborating with Facing History to create safer, more reflective environments.

We also acknowledge the valuable support we've received on this project from educators. We extend our gratitude to: Katya Babitskaya, Angela Corbet, Denny Conklin, Kathryn DeWitt, Paul DiPietro, Katy Frost, Lori Hodin, Karen Kennedy, Karen Langlais, Josh Otlin and Jose Valenzuela.

We rely on the collaboration of reviewers to reinforce our approach to the guide's content. With sincere gratitude, we acknowledge: Maureen Costello, Director, Teaching Tolerance; Alan Heisterkamp, Ed.D., President, Cultivating Minds, and Director of the MVP Leadership Institute at the Center for Violence Prevention; Stephanie Jones, Assistant Professor of Education, Harvard Graduate School of Education; Jennifer Hoos Rothberg, Executive Director, Einhorn Family Charitable Trust; Katie Smith, BeCause Foundation; Lisa Thomas, Ed.D., Associate Director, Educational Issues Department, American Federation of Teachers; Emily Verellen, Director of Programs and Communications, The Fledgling Fund; and Richard Weissbourd, Ed.D., Director, Human Development and Psychology Program, Harvard Graduate School of Education.

Developing this guide required efforts of individuals throughout the organization. We deeply appreciate the Facing History and Ourselves staff for their time and for their editorial contributions that made this resource more engaging. We are especially grateful to Margot Stern Strom, Marc Skvirsky, Marty Sleeper, Adam Strom, Fran Colletti, Dennis Barr, Jennifer Jones-Clark, Dimitry Anselme, Karen Barss, Liz Kelleher, John Englander, Jocelyn Stanton, Anne Burt, and Catherine O'Keefe.

Table of Contents

Using Film as a Catalyst for Change

By Marty Sleeper, Associate Executive Director,
Facing History and Ourselves

BULLY provides a compelling and tragic portrait of the consequences of bullying in our society. Like the phenomenon of bullying itself, the film is direct and hard-hitting. Through the power of individual stories, the film aims to be a catalyst for change in the way we deal with bullying as parents, teachers, children, and society as a whole. The purpose of this guide is to help adult and student audiences confront the stories told in the film and explore their meaning and resonance for their schools and wider communities. Careful preparation by educators who intend to use the film with their students is not only critical, but will pay off in precipitating the kind of honest, open discussion about caring and responsibility that the film is designed to engender.

At Facing History and Ourselves, we have spent over 35 years researching, teaching, and writing about historical episodes of collective violence in which the marginalization and humiliation of particular groups played the central role. Seemingly small steps of ridicule and labeling, when allowed to persist and go unchallenged, have too often had catastrophic consequences. Why, in such cases, did some people willingly conform to the norms of a group, even when those norms encouraged wrongdoing, while others spoke out and resisted? That is a Facing History and Ourselves question that might well be on the minds of viewers of this film. It is part of the intellectual and pedagogical framework developed by Facing History, which not only focuses on how history informs the present, but also helps young people look at difficult events and find connections to their own lives. That framework further encompasses concepts and vocabulary that are familiar to adolescents: identity, membership, stereotyping, conformity, peer pressure, leading and following, in-groups and out-groups, judgment, and responsibility. Having students use such terms as a lens through which to view and discuss the stories in the film will encourage them to make connections between more extreme situations and less serious actions and behavior that they participate in or observe in their everyday lives.

The necessity of adults previewing the full film before using it with young people cannot be overemphasized. Ideally, that would be done with a group of faculty and school personnel, including counselors. In any case, it is important that adults take the time to reflect upon their reactions to the film, and many of the suggestions in this guide will assist in that process. When using the film with students, adults need to anticipate and prepare for how young people will respond. Initially, there can be a wide range of responses—silence, blaming victims, discomfort that shows itself in joking and laughter—as well as an insistence that it has nothing to do with their lives. On the other hand, some students may see the film as hitting particularly close to home, and need individual support. But engendering the kind of classroom atmosphere of trust, respect for different opinions, and honest, informed discussion that is described in the opening section of the guide will best facilitate moving on and thinking together about actions that sustain an environment in which bullying of any sort is simply not acceptable.

Preventing bullying in our schools and communities will not be a quick fix or simple solution. Stopping it needs to go far beyond reacting to alarming media headlines, completing surveys, and distributing zero-tolerance policy reminders—as important as all of that may be. In the best schools, every adult, no matter what his or her position or job title, recognizes and accepts his or her responsibility as role model and educator. Every adult takes the matter of bullying seriously, and sees it as his or her responsibility to prevent it when possible and intervene if it arises. Explicit curricula and non-curricular programs foster social and emotional competencies, such as perspective-taking and empathy, which make bullying less likely. The entire school community is alert to signals and warning signs and everyone finds a way to "upstand" on behalf of the safe and respectful learning and living environment that every young person deserves. That hope lies behind the film and all of the suggested thinking and activity in this guide.

How to Use This Guide

We anticipate that the film BULLY will inspire reflection and discussion among a variety of audiences. We have designed this guide to be used both by facilitators working with the adult members of a school community, as well as by faculty members who would like to use the film to foster discussion with students. Therefore, the suitability of many of the materials included here will depend significantly on your goals, the age group of your audience, and the familiarity that your audience has with the topic of bullying.

This guide is divided into four sections: **Pre-Viewing, Post-Viewing, Continuing the Conversation,** and **Discussion Strategies.**

The **Pre-Viewing** section includes three readings designed to introduce the concept of bullying, provide some general information about its prevalence, and build some understanding of its causes, effects, and complexity before you show the film. This section also provides a brief preview of each story in the film with guiding questions to help viewers begin to process the film as they view it.

The **Post-Viewing** section includes several readings that explore themes such as friendship, adult intervention, and upstanders and bystanders. The readings in this section focus on specific scenes in the film, and they are designed to help viewers process some of the film's challenging, personal moments. Each reading also draws on recent scholarship and expert perspectives to build an intellectual framework for understanding the experiences of the young people and adults portrayed in the film.

The **Continuing the Conversation** section includes a more in-depth activity, developed by Facing History and Ourselves, that you may decide to use in your school community. Entitled "Bullying: A Case Study in Ostracism," this module can be used with both students and adults. An abridged version is included here along with a link to the full case study, which is available on the Facing History and Ourselves website.

The **Discussion Strategies** section is an appendix of strategies and activities that Facing History and Ourselves has found effective in facilitating meaningful discussions about sensitive topics. The emphasis in all of these discussion strategies is on making sure that every voice is heard and valued. The research on bullying tells us that it is in just these types of environments that bullying is least likely to take hold. The strategies are written for teachers to use with students, but it is our experience that they are effective with groups of adults as well. Many of the readings throughout this guide are followed by *Classroom Suggestions,* which reference specific discussion strategies from this section. Please keep in mind that these are only suggestions; each teacher and facilitator knows his or her audience best.

Finally, most of the readings in this guide include **Connections.** These questions explore and extend the themes in the readings. It is not expected that you will discuss every question with your class or group. You might find that some are suitable to use with students while others are best used with groups of adults. It is essential that you, as the teacher or facilitator, determine which **Connections** questions will be most useful for the audience with which you are working.

ON THE WEB

This guide is part of a larger collection of resources about bullying and ostracism that Facing History and Ourselves has compiled online. The collection is available at *www.facinghistory.org/safeschools.*

Visit *www.thebullyproject.com* for additional resources including tips for parents, students, and school staff on taking steps to help prevent bullying and to create a climate in schools in which students can feel safe.

Creating a Safe and Reflective Environment

Recent research suggests that bullying is less prevalent in school communities and classrooms that have democratic cultures and value student voices.[1] These findings are consistent with Facing History and Ourselves philosophy of creating a reflective classroom community. We believe that a Facing History and Ourselves classroom is in many ways a microcosm of democracy—a place where explicit rules and implicit norms protect everyone's right to speak; where different perspectives can be heard and valued; where members take responsibility for themselves, each other, and the group as a whole; and where each member has a stake and a voice in collective decisions. We extend this philosophy to the adult learning communities in which we participate. It stands to reason that, in order to facilitate meaningful discussion, improve school climate, and reduce bullying, we must foster the characteristics of a reflective, democratic learning community.

As you plan your approach to viewing and discussing BULLY with your school community, faculty and staff, parents, or students, it is essential to nurture a reflective environment by

- creating a sense of trust and openness;
- encouraging participants to speak and listen to one another;
- making space and time for silent reflection;
- offering multiple avenues for participation and learning; and
- helping students appreciate the points of view, talents, and contributions of less vocal members.

We have found success by emphasizing journal writing and employing multiple formats for facilitating large and small group discussions. In the **Discussion Strategies** section at the end of this guide, we have provided a collection of discussion strategies that we have found effective in ensuring that every voice is heard and valued.

Finally, we recommend that, before viewing and discussing BULLY, you first create a group contract with those who will participate, be they adults or children. Contracts typically include several clearly defined rules or expectations for participation, and consequences for those who do not fulfill their obligations as members of the learning community. There are a variety of ways to go about creating a contract. A sample contract is provided below. You might choose to present it to the members of your community before viewing and discussing the film, making sure to have them affirm their agreement to each guideline. Then invite the group to discuss or amend any parts of the contract before continuing.

Sample Community Contract:

- Listen with respect. Try to understand what someone is saying before rushing to judgment.
- Make comments using "I" statements.
- If you do not feel safe making a comment or asking a question, write the thought down.
- If someone states an idea or question that helps your own learning, say, "Thank you."
- If someone says something that hurts or offends you, do not attack the person. Acknowledge that the comment—not the person—hurt your feelings and explain why.
- Put-downs are never okay.
- If you don't understand something, ask a question.
- Think with your head and your heart.
- Share talking time—provide room for others to speak.
- Do not interrupt others while they are speaking.
- Write down thoughts, in a journal or notebook, if you don't have time to say them during our time together.

Notes

1 Philip C. Rodkin, "Bullying and Children's Peer Relationships," in *White House Conference on Bullying Prevention*, 36–37, accessed October 18, 2011, http://stopbullying.gov/references/white_house_conference/index.html.

PRE-VIEWING

Unlike many documentaries, BULLY does not include any analysis of the events that are portrayed on film. There is no narrator to provide context, no experts to explain the psychology of those who bully or are bullied.

According to Lee Hirsch, the director of the film, the absence of analysis was intentional. Instead, he set out to create a film that is "undeniable and emotional" to serve as a starting point for conversations about combating bullying.[1]

One of the goals of this guide is to help facilitate that conversation and provide much of the context, analysis, and intellectual framework that Hirsch chose not to include in the film. The Pre-Viewing section starts this process.

Lee Hirsch/The Weinstein Company

This section includes three readings:

1. **"BULLY: The Stories in the Film"** (pp. 11–14) introduces each of the film's subjects and provides guiding questions to help frame viewers' thinking as they watch.

2. **"What Is Bullying?"** (pp. 15–16) provides definitions, statistics, and other general background information from recent research on bullying and its effects. Instead of reading this information with students, teachers may choose to have their students create and discuss their own definitions of bullying.

3. **"The 'In' Group"** (pp. 17–18) is a first-hand account of an incident of ostracism from a middle school classroom. This story is offered in addition to the stories told in the film because it raises valuable questions for students and adults to consider before watching.

Notes

1 Lee Hirsch, interview by author, telephone, October 13, 2011.

BULLY: The Stories in the Film

BULLY follows five stories of children and families who are affected deeply by bullying over the course of a school year. With intimate glimpses into homes, classrooms, cafeterias, and principals' offices, the film offers insight into the often cruel world of bullied children. As teachers, administrators, kids, and parents struggle to find answers to this cruelty, BULLY examines the dire consequences of bullying through the testimony of courageous youth.

Viewers of all ages will likely have personal reactions to the challenging stories in this film. These stories include two families who have lost children to suicide and a mother waiting to know the fate of her 14-year-old daughter who has been incarcerated after bringing a gun on her school bus to confront her tormentors. It is essential that adults not only view BULLY before showing it to adolescents but also take time to think about their own personal responses to these stories. Adults should think carefully about how to prepare young people for the emotional reactions the film will elicit. Adults should also be aware that the film contains profanity and explicit violence.

Brief previews of each of the stories are provided on the following pages. They are formatted for photocopying so that you may distribute them to viewers for reference while watching the film. Regardless of the audience, but especially for adolescent viewers, we suggest reading these previews together before viewing. Each story is accompanied by a set of guiding questions. You may choose to use these guiding questions to begin your discussion after the film. Note, however, that the questions are designed to anticipate issues that will be raised in the *Post-Viewing* section of this guide.

Classroom Suggestions

You may choose to have students create *Identity Charts* (page 48) for themselves and one or more of the young people they watch in the film. Identity charts help students consider the many factors that shape each person's identity. By comparing their own identity charts with those they made for people in the film, students may begin to make more explicit connections with those victimized by bullying. They may also begin to appreciate the differences that exist in their community that might make one more vulnerable to being bullied. Students can start to draw the identity charts based on the information in the previews below. They can then add to the charts either while watching the film or afterward.

BULLY: Story Synopses[1]

The Longs
Chattsworth, Georgia

"From the day Tyler was born, I was probably the proudest dad in the world. Because he was the firstborn; he was the first son. He always had that laugh about him, I don't know, it was infectious, it caught you."

After years of relentless bullying, on October 17th, 2009, Tyler Long was found hanging in his closet. Tina and David Long mourn the loss of their son, whom they tried to protect, and they take to task the school system that failed him so miserably. Tyler's death sparks debate in the community, played out in public forums and town hall meetings, as the community is forced to face its bullying demons.

"Tyler wasn't the most athletic," his dad says. "When he was in PE, he was always the last one to be [chosen]. Nobody would be on his team, because they said he was a geek and a fag and they didn't want to play with him. And it took a toll on him early in middle school. To where he, he cried, and then it got to the point where he didn't cry anymore. And that's when it became difficult to truly understand what he was going through."

Guiding Questions

As you watch the film, what does the Longs' story make you think about and feel? Who bears responsibility for the effects of bullying?

What can we learn from the parents of a bullied child? How might they make a positive difference in their community?

How should communities respond to suicides by young people who are bullied? How can they protect young people from the despair caused by bullying?

Alex, 14
Sioux City, Iowa

"I feel good when I'm in this house and when I'm with my family. Maya, my sister, she is annoying, but that's normal for a sister. Then there's Ethan, he's my six-year-old brother. He got all A's in preschool through kindergarten. I'm proud of him for that. Then there's Jada, she talks a lot. Then there's Logan, my two-year-old brother, then my mama and my dad. And then there's me."

Alex has spent the summer trying not to think about what might happen when he returns to school, where for years he's been punched, choked, sat on, had things stolen from him, and called names. Alex has Asperger's Syndrome, an autism spectrum disorder that often affects one's social interactions. Feeling powerless to stop his torment at school, Alex is forced to worry about his role as a big brother when his younger sister enters the middle school the following school year. As Alex endures another school year of being bullied, his parents struggle to get him to talk to them about his experiences at school, and they are unsettled by the school's inability to keep him safe.

"I feel kind of nervous going back to school cause . . . I like learning, but I have trouble making friends," Alex says as the summer ends. "People think that I'm different, I'm not normal. Most kids don't want to be around me. I feel like I belong somewhere else."

Guiding Questions

As you watch the film, what does Alex's story make you think about and feel? How do people respond when they encounter a difference that they do not understand?

What can parents and school officials do to help a child who is bullied? What kind of responses by adults can help and what kind might make matters worse? When is adult intervention most helpful?

Kelby, 16
Tuttle, Oklahoma

"You know what my philosophy about rain is? You know when people can't hold it anymore, they cry? The world is taking so much in, it can't hold anymore. That's why it rains. Because it's letting go."

 After Kelby came out as gay, teachers and administrators turned a blind eye when she was beat up by boys in between classes and run down by a carful of classmates, puncturing the windshield with her head. Though her parents have offered to move to another town, Kelby returns to school in the fall filled with determination to stand up to her tormentors—and graduate with honors. As much as she is buoyed by a small group of friends, her determination is challenged throughout the year by students and adults alike.

"You can always count on something happening when you're walking down the hall at school, in the classroom, after school when I'm walking home, when I'm walking through the parking lot in the morning to school. I wasn't welcomed at church. I'm not welcomed in a lot of people's homes. I know [my friends] get called gay just for hanging out with me."

Guiding Questions

As you watch the film, what does Kelby's story make you think about and feel? What are the sources of Kelby's strength and optimism? How is she able to face the bullying she endures with such determination?

Why are LGBT (lesbian, gay, bisexual, and transgender) youth so often singled out for bullying and harassment in middle and high school? How does bullying reflect larger societal conflicts and attitudes?

Ja'Meya, 14
Yazoo County, Mississippi

Looking around Ja'Meya's bedroom, her mother says, "This is her comfort zone, to herself. She was a basketball player. These are her trophies, her awards. Got her names on 'em and everything. She was an honor student. Yeah, she is an honor student. She said when she finished school, she want to go to the navy . . . Because she didn't want to see me work so hard. She wanted to help me out."

 Despite being an athlete and a top student, Ja'Meya was picked on every morning and afternoon of her hour-long bus ride through Mississippi. "It all started back when school first began and there was a lot of kids on the bus saying things about me," she explains. "I tried my best to tell an adult, but it got worse." Ja'Meya finally had enough. On the bus, she took out the gun she found in her mother's closet. Although no one on the bus was harmed, Ja'Meya was arrested and charged with 45 felony accounts, enough to send her to prison for a hundred years.

As they wait for the criminal justice system to determine her fate, Ja'Meya's family struggles to understand how she could have become so desperate. In custody, Ja'Meya tries to come to terms with the consequences of her actions, and she misses her home terribly.

Guiding Questions

As you watch the film, what does Ja'Meya's story make you think about and feel? As an athlete and an honor student, how does Ja'Meya defy your assumptions about the victims of bullying? How do you know who is most vulnerable?

How do you explain Ja'Meya's decision to bring a gun on the school bus? What do you think should be the consequences for her action? Does it matter that she did not intend to hurt anyone? What, if any, lessons can we draw from her story?

Ja'Meya is African American. How might race influence the way that people respond to her story? How might it influence your understanding of the situation?

The Smalleys
Perkins, Oklahoma

"We'd go and work on our clubhouse," says Trey, Ty Field-Smalley's best friend. "It's way back out in the woods and no one but me and Ty knows where it is. We would just entertain ourselves for about five hours, it would feel like 30 minutes. Just hanging out, having a good time. Ty was just the coolest kid I knew."

 At age 11, Ty took his own life after being bullied repeatedly. "Even when people would bully him, I'd get so angry, and I could have hurt those kids so badly that done something to him," says Trey. "Like they'll push him down, and say, 'Shut up spaz,' or throw him into a locker, or shove him into one. And I'd just go to take off after them and he'd be like, 'Trey, it isn't worth it, be better than them, it's all right,' and he'd walk off with a smile. And I don't know how he could do it. He was way stronger than I was."

Ty's suicide has motivated his parents to create the organization Stand for the Silent, to empower students to stop bullying. Ty's father, Kirk Smalley, has vowed, "I'll fight bullying wherever it's found. Schools. Workplace. I'm not going to quit until bullying does."

Guiding Questions

As you watch the film, what does the Smalleys' story make you think about and feel?

How important are friends in the life of one who is bullied? How can friends help? How much power do individuals, and individual families, have to create change in our society?

Notes

1 BULLY, directed by Lee Hirsch, 2011.

What Is Bullying?

> [I]f it involves repeated, malicious attempts to
> humiliate a helpless victim, if the victim is fearful, does
> not know how to make it stop, then it's bullying.[1]
> —Kim Zarzour

Kim Zarzour, an education journalist, points to the two key characteristics—repeated harmful acts and an imbalance of power—that most experts agree separate bullying from other conflicts that arise among young people.

Bullying involves an individual or a group repeatedly harming another person—physically (e.g., punching, pushing, tripping, or destruction of property), verbally (e.g., teasing, name-calling, or intimidating), or socially (e.g., ostracizing or spreading hurtful rumors).[2] Sometimes these harmful actions are plainly visible, but other times, such as when gossip and rumors are used to isolate the target, the actions are covert. With the advent of the Internet, bullies are able to maintain a more persistent presence in the lives of their victims through cyberbullying. Researchers define cyberbullying as "willful and repeated harm inflicted through the use of computers, cell phones, and other electronic devices."[3]

Researchers note that bullying often does not happen in an isolated context with a single tormentor and victim. There may be multiple bullies or multiple victims, and there are almost always peers, adults, and other community members who know about the bullying. Often, the victims of bullying are socially vulnerable because they have some characteristic that makes them different from the majority. A person might be singled out because of his or her race, ethnicity, sexual orientation, or religious affiliation. Young people who have physical or learning disabilities are also targeted more frequently, as well as students who are on the autism spectrum.[4] Other times, there are no apparent characteristics that cause the target of bullying to be singled out by the tormentor. Regardless, the person being bullied does not know how, or does not have the power, to make it stop.

While bullying occurs across all grade levels, researchers point out that it is most prevalent in middle school and remains common throughout high school.

- In 2011, two-thirds of middle school faculty and staff reported that they witnessed bullying frequently in their schools.[5]
- A few years earlier, 89% of middle school students interviewed had witnessed an act of bullying and 49% said they had been a victim of a bully.[6]
- In 2009, 20% of high school students reported being bullied at school during the previous twelve months.[7]
- The National Association of School Psychologists estimates that over 160,000 students miss school each day because they fear being bullied.[8]

With increasing frequency, bullying is making the headlines due to stories about its severe effects on children and families. The recent stream of news stories about the victims of bullying committing suicide

Classroom Suggestions

Teachers may decide to use this reading as background information for themselves and, instead of reading it in class, ask their students to construct their own definitions of bullying.

Once students have created their definitions, they can share and discuss them using the *Think, Pair, Share* strategy (page 52). By the end of the discussion, the teacher should emphasize the two key characteristics of bullying: repeated harmful acts and an imbalance of power.

underscores the serious potential consequences that arise from this behavior. Psychologists observe that sometimes the targets of bullying turn inward in response to their torment and sometimes they channel their pain and frustration outward toward others.

The effects of turning inward, what psychologists call an *internalized response,* include depression and anxiety. Studies link those who are bullied to above average levels of depression and anxiety as well as diminished performance in school.[9] Research also suggests that young people who are bullied are significantly more likely than others to have suicidal thoughts. It is important to note that those who bully are also more likely to suffer from depression, anxiety, and suicidal thoughts than those uninvolved in bullying.[10]

The effects of turning outward, what psychologists call an *externalized response,* include various forms of aggressive behavior. Sometimes those who are bullied respond by threatening, intimidating, or bullying others. This is common enough that many researchers refer to *bullies, victims,* and a third category, *bully-victims.* Those who bully others are also, themselves, at increased risk for substance abuse, academic problems, and violence later in adolescence and adulthood.[11]

Connections

1. Researchers measure and define bullying in different ways. How do you define bullying? Is the description of bullying in this reading adequate? At what point does conflict between students become bullying? At what point do you think the adults in a school community should take particular conflicts between students more seriously? As you watch and think about the film, you may choose to modify your definition of bullying.

2. How do the statistics included here help define the scope of the bullying problem? Which statistics do you find most striking? What questions do they raise?

3. In one recent study, 20% of respondents aged 11–18 said they had been a victim of cyberbullying at some point in their life.[12] In what ways is cyberbullying similar to other forms of bullying? In what ways is it different? How does cyberbullying present new challenges for students and for schools? To what extent do you think that schools have a responsibility to deal with cyberbullies?

4. Research shows that many of the victims of bullying are singled out because of race, ethnicity, sexual orientation, religion, or physical or learning disabilities. What are some reasons people might respond to such differences so hurtfully? Why do some differences lead to ridicule more than others?

Notes

1 Kim Zarzour, *Facing the Schoolyard Bully: How to Raise an Assertive Child in an Aggressive World* (Buffalo, New York: Firefly Books, 2000), 24.

2 Jing Wang, Ronald J. Iannotti, and Tonja R. Nansel, "School Bullying Among Adolescents in the United States: Physical, Verbal, Relational, and Cyber," *Journal of Adolescent Health* 45, no. 4 (October 2009): 368–69, accessed October 20, 2011, doi:10.1016/j.jadohealth.2009.03.021.

3 Sameer Hunduja and Justin W. Patchin, "Overview of Cyberbullying," in *White House Conference on Bullying Prevention,* 21, accessed October 18, 2011, http://www.stopbullying.gov/references/white_house_conference/index.html.

4 Susan M. Swearer, "Risk Factors for and Outcomes of Bullying and Victimization," in *White House Conference on Bullying Prevention,* 3–5, accessed October 18, 2011, http://www.stopbullying.gov/references/white_house_conference/index.html.

5 Michaela Gulemetova, Darrel Drury, and Catherine P. Bradshaw, "Findings From the National Education Association's Nationwide Study of Bullying: Teachers' and Education Support Professionals' Perspectives," in *White House Conference on Bullying Prevention,* 12, accessed October 18, 2011, http://www.stopbullying.gov/references/white_house_conference/index.html.

6 F. Pergolizzi et al., "Bullying in middle school: Results from a 2008 survey," Abstract, *International Journal of Adolescent Medicine and Health* (2011), accessed October 20, 2011, http://www.ncbi.nlm.nih.gov/pubmed/21721358.

7 Understanding Bullying: Fact Sheet 2011 (National Center for Injury Prevention and Control: Division of Violence Prevention, 2011), accessed October 19, 2011, http://www.cdc.gov/ViolencePrevention/pdf/Bullying_Factsheet-a.pdf.

8 Swearer, "Risk Factors," 7.

9 Ibid.

10 "Bullying–Suicide Link Explored in New Study by Researchers at Yale," *YaleNews,* July 16, 2008, accessed October 19, 2011, http://news.yale.edu/2008/07/16/bullying-suicide-link-explored-new-study-researchers-yale.

11 Swearer, "Risk Factors," 4–7.

12 Hunduja and Patchin, "Overview," 21.

The "In" Group

Bullying can take many forms beyond the particularly severe examples portrayed in the film BULLY. Bullies may also use ostracism and social exclusion, without inflicting any physical harm, to isolate the students they target. This type of behavior is called *relational bullying*. While sometimes less obvious than physical bullying, relational bullying can cause just as much pain.

When bullying occurs, regardless of its form, peers play a powerful role. All humans yearn to belong, and throughout our lives we define ourselves, in large part, by the groups to which we belong. Of course, the group that first shapes our identity is our family. As we become adolescents, however, our peers begin to play an extremely important role in how we define ourselves and in the decisions we make.[1]

Researchers consider bullying a social event, meaning that it involves many more people—including peers, educators, and parents—other than the tormentor and the target. In most cases, bullying takes place in the presence of others, but even peers who are not present are often aware that it is happening. As a result, the responses of peers can have a significant effect on the behavior of those who bully. Witnesses of bullying can choose to join in the bullying behavior, to be *bystanders* and do nothing, or to be *upstanders* and try to find a way to help the target.

Eve S., a high-school student, describes a time when she witnessed the exclusion of one of her classmates and she faced this choice:

> My eighth grade consisted of 28 students, most of whom knew each other from the age of five or six. The class was close-knit and we knew each other so well that most of us could distinguish each other's handwriting at a glance. Although we grew up together, we still had class outcasts. From second grade on, a small elite group spent a large portion of their time harassing two or three of the others. I was one of those two or three, though I don't know why. In most cases when children get picked on, they aren't good at sports or they read too much or they wear the wrong clothes or they are of a different race. But in my class, we all read too much and didn't know how to play sports. We had also been brought up to carefully respect each other's races. This is what was so strange about my situation. Usually, people are made outcasts because they are in some way different from the larger group. But in my class, large differences did not exist. It was as if the outcasts were invented by the group out of a need for them. Differences between us did not cause hatred; hatred caused differences between us.

> The harassment was subtle. It came in the form of muffled giggles when I talked, and rolled eyes when I turned around. If I was out in the playground and approached a group of people, they often fell silent. Sometimes someone would not see me coming and I would catch the tail end of a joke at my expense.

> I also have a memory of a different kind. There was another girl in our class who was perhaps even more rejected than I. She also tried harder than I did for acceptance, providing the group with ample material for jokes. One day during lunch I was sitting outside watching a basketball game. One of the popular girls in the class came up to me to show me something she said I wouldn't want to miss. We walked to a corner of the playground where a group of three or four sat. One of them read aloud from a small book, which I was told was the girl's diary. I sat down and, laughing till my sides hurt, heard my voice finally blend with the others. Looking back, I wonder how I could have participated in mocking this girl when I knew perfectly well what it felt like to be mocked myself. I would like to say that if I were in that situation today I would react differently, but I can't honestly be sure. Often being accepted by others is more satisfying than being accepted by oneself, even though the satisfaction does not last. Too often our actions are determined by the moment.[2]

Classroom Suggestions

Eve's story contains several powerful and provocative statements about human behavior. You might ask students to choose a phrase or sentence that stands out to them from her story as the basis for a *Think, Pair, Share* (page 52) discussion. You can continue the discussion using Connections questions from above.

Connections

1. How is ostracism similar to and different from other forms of bullying? When does ostracizing, or excluding someone from a group, become bullying?

2. How does Eve's story relate to bullying? Was she bullied? Did she bully? How would you explain her behavior in this story?

3. Psychologists Michael Thompson and Lawrence Cohen point to the powerful influence of peer groups in guiding our behavior. They write:

    We all know that groups can go terribly astray in terms of their moral reasoning. Everyone not in the group can be considered an outsider, a legitimate target. . . . [I]t affects every group, because we are all prone to that feeling of us versus them and the idea that if you're not with us you're against us. Speaking out against a risky, immoral, or illegal decision is hard to do because that makes you an outsider yourself.[3]

    How did Eve's need to belong affect the way she responded when another girl was mocked? Why does her response still trouble her? How do you like to think you would have responded to the incident?

4. What language should we use when discussing those who are involved in or affected by bullying? What does it mean to label someone as a *bully?* What does it mean to label someone as a *victim?* Can the same person be a bully and a victim in different situations?

5. Many times, those who are bullied are singled out because of some difference—such as sexual orientation, race, or disability—that separates them from the majority. However, Eve says that the members of her small class did not have any such differences. She writes, "It was as if the outcasts were invented by the group out of a need for them. Differences between us did not cause hatred; hatred caused differences between us."

    How does her observation change how you think about bullying and ostracism? What do you think is at the root of bullying behavior?

6. Eve concludes, "Often being accepted by others is more satisfying than being accepted by oneself, even though the satisfaction does not last." What does she mean?

7. To what extent can the behavior of adults be affected by a need to be part of the "In" group? How might educators' responses to bullying and ostracism be affected by the popularity of the students involved?

Notes

1 Jing Wang, Ronald J. Iannotti, and Tonja R. Nansel, "School Bullying Among Adolescents in the United States: Physical, Verbal, Relational, and Cyber," *Journal of Adolescent Health 45*, no. 4 (October 2009): 368–69, accessed October 20, 2011, doi:10.1016/j.jadohealth.2009.03.021.

2 Margot Stern Strom, *Facing History and Ourselves: Holocaust and Human Behavior,* (Brookline: Facing History and Ourselves National Foundation, Inc., 1994), 29.

3 Michael Thompson Ph.D., Lawrence J. Cohen Ph.D., and Catherine O'Neill Grace, *Mom, They're Teasing Me: Helping Your Child Solve Social Problems* (New York: Ballantine Books, 2002), 71.

POST-VIEWING

BULLY often elicits powerful reactions from viewers. Chief among these is sadness and frustration over the intensity of the torment the film portrays. Viewers are also often left with a sense of puzzlement about both the ineffective responses of so many people in the film and the lack of safety for those who are victimized.

This section is designed to help viewers begin to process these reactions by analyzing excerpts and quotations from the film. Another goal of this section is to continue to build understanding and foster discussion of the various causes and effects of bullying behavior. It is from this foundation of understanding and difficult discussion that school communities can begin to take the first steps towards effectively combating bullying.

Lee Hirsch/The Weinstein Company

This section includes seven readings that explore a variety of themes present in the film:

- **"Experiencing Bullying"** (pp. 20–22) prompts readers to reflect on the pain and isolation felt by young people who are bullied.

- **"Telling the Stories"** (pp. 23–25) includes an interview with the filmmaker, providing important details about the rationale for the film and how it was made.

- **"The Power of Friends"** (pp. 26–27) explores the important role that friendship can play in the life of a young person who is bullied.

- **"Upstanders and Bystanders"** (pp. 28–29) encourages readers to consider the variety of ways they can help those who are bullied.

- **"The Impact on Parents"** (pp. 30–31) explores how parents respond when they have a child who is bullied.

- **"Adult Intervention"** (pp. 32–35) considers helpful actions that educators and other adults can take to respond to and prevent bullying, as well as the types of responses that can make matters worse.

- **"Nurturing School Culture"** (pp. 36–39) examines the relationship between bullying and school culture, and prompts readers to think about how to make their schools more caring and supportive environments.

Experiencing Bullying

BULLY tells raw and powerful stories about bullying and the effects it has on the lives of victims and their families. "It is critical that the film reveals the true darkness that is bullying," explains director Lee Hirsch. "We don't have a way to say how destructive this is." He hopes the film will help people understand the devastation caused by bullying.

Hirsch says that he chose to exclude analysis from the film. "Instead we thought, 'Let's create something undeniable and emotional.'" Hirsch intends for the movie to serve as a starting point for conversation and a catalyst for developing more effective strategies for combating bullying.[1]

Lee Hirsch/The Weinstein Company

The stories in the film are especially poignant because they are told in the words of those most affected by bullying:

Alex

"They punch me in the jaw, strangle me, they knock things out of my hand, take things from me, sit on me. They push me so far that, that I want to become the bully."

Ja'Meya

"It feels like everybody just turned against me. It was like nine of them, nine or ten of them, calling me stupid and dumb, and they started throwing things at me, and one of the guys said something to me, and he threatened me, telling me what he was going to do to me, and he'll fight girls, and everybody was laughing. And I was telling him to be quiet, and he kept talking and that's when I got up."

Kelby

"Yeah, you know, I went in thinking it was going to be a new year, and people were used to me. And I went into class, and the class was already full, and I sat down, and everyone around me moved seats. Like every single person. I was the only one sitting in a little circle. That was enough. Maybe there's another place I can try to make a difference."

David Long

". . . [W]e knew why Tyler did what he did. There was no doubt in our minds. When you're in the shower and your clothes are taken, and you have no way of getting out of the gym other than walking out naked. When you're standing in the bathroom urinating, and kids come up and push you from behind up against the stall and against the wall, and you urinate on your pants. When you're sitting in the classroom and someone grabs your books and throws them on the floor and tells you, 'Pick 'em up bitch,' those are things that happened to Tyler. Did he ever come home with blood running down his face? No. It was the mental abuse and the not so physical abuse that Tyler endured. . . . He had a target on his back, everybody knew that."[2]

Classroom Suggestions

The *Save the Last Word for Me* strategy (page 54) provides an effective format for encouraging every student to think deeply about the experiences of those who are bullied in the film. The structure that this strategy puts in place facilitates careful listening and ensures that every voice is heard.

Connections

1. Which parts of the film had the greatest impact on you?

2. Pointing to the prevalence of journals, blogs, and videos posted online by victims of bullying, Hirsch observes a universal feeling: "Kids who are bullied want to have a voice."[3] In what ways are the voices of young people who are bullied diminished or ignored in our society? How does BULLY amplify the voices of those who are bullied?

3. What is *empathy?* How does the film help us build empathy for the targets of bullying? How might increasing empathy help a community reduce the amount of bullying that occurs?

4. Hirsch chose to focus the film solely on the stories of those who are victimized by bullying. What might we learn about bullying from their stories? What might we learn from experts? What other perspectives would be helpful?

5. BULLY does not provide any stories or details about the students who behave as bullies. Why do you think that the filmmaker chose not to include the bully's perspective?

6. Define *courage* and *resilience*. In what ways are the young people we meet in this film courageous? In what ways are they resilient? What is the difference between the two?

7. Recent insights from neuroscience suggest that the distress caused by social exclusion or disapproval activates the same regions of the brain that are active when one feels physical pain. In other words, the body responds to physical and emotional pain similarly.[4] How might these findings deepen our understanding of and empathy for victims of bullying?

8. Although the fact is not shared in the film, Alex has Asperger's Syndrome. Tyler Long had it, too. People with Asperger's, an autism spectrum disorder, often have difficulty perceiving nonverbal social cues and expressing empathy. How might this disorder make one more vulnerable to bullying and harassment?

    Unlike many physical disabilities, Asperger's Syndrome is not a condition that is immediately visible to others. How might the visibility of one's disability change how he or she is treated by others?

9. Hirsch says that he chose not to reveal in the film that Alex and Tyler have Asperger's because he did not want to provide the audience with easy excuses for their victimization. "We didn't want anything to make the audience think, 'Oh, well that explains it, well of course,'"[5] he says. What other types of easy excuses might people make when explaining why certain people are the victims of bullying?

10. In the excerpt above, Alex shares, "They push me so far that, that I want to become the bully." Although Alex does not become a bully, many bullying targets share his sentiment. How do you explain Alex's desire to bully?

    Researchers estimate that from one-third to one-half of those who bully are bullied as well.[6] This group is often referred to as *bully-victims,* those who are bullies to some and targets of bullying by others. What does the existence of bully-victims suggest about the nature of bullying? Is Eve S. (from "The 'In' Group") a bully-victim? What might motivate one who is a victim of bullying to torment others?

11. Hirsch wonders why our society allows young people to torment each other in ways that would never be acceptable among adults:

    How much abuse is too much when bullying is involved? When does the assault reach a threshold where it's too much in society's viewpoint? If an adult was to strike another adult twice, that adult would be in jail. You would have a restraining order, society would say that's not acceptable. But some of these kids endure what amounts to torture. The daily abuse is significant. So when we talk about Ja'Meya, it's a delicate conversation to have because obviously you don't want to send the message that if you are being bullied you can pull a gun out, but [where] does a kid who's not getting help from adults or from her peers. . . turn to? Sadly one of the other places they turn to is suicide, when they feel like they can get no relief.[7]

Do you agree with Hirsch that bullying is as serious as assault and abuse between adults? When young people are getting bullied, whom can they turn to for support? How do you explain why they do not always get the support they need?

Notes

1 Lee Hirsch, interview by author, telephone, October 13, 2011.

2 BULLY, directed by Lee Hirsch, 2011.

3 Lee Hirsch, interview by author, telephone, October 13, 2011.

4 Tracy Vaillancourt, Shelley Hymel, and Patricia McDougall, "Why does being bullied hurt so much?: Insights from Neuroscience" (2004), in *Bullying in North American Schools,* ed. Dorothy L. Espelage and Susan M. Swearer, 2nd ed. (New York: Routledge, 2011), 26–28.

5 Lee Hirsch, interview by author, telephone, October 13, 2011.

6 Rene Veenstra et al., "Bullying and Victimization in Elementary Schools: A Comparison of Bullies, Victims, Bully/Victims, and Uninvolved Preadolescents," *Developmental Psychology* 41, no. 4 (2005): 673, accessed October 25, 2011, http://www.gmw.rug.nl/~veenstra/CV/TRAILS_Veenstra_DP05.pdf.

7 Lee Hirsch, interview by author, telephone, October 13, 2011.

Telling the Stories

Making BULLY involved more than a year of following stories and shooting footage in several schools and communities around the United States. Much of what director Lee Hirsch captured on film did not make it into the final version of the film. As with many documentaries, making BULLY involved making difficult choices about what to include and what to leave out. In a conversation with Facing History and Ourselves, Hirsch reflected on the stories he documented and how he decided what to include in the film.[1]

Facing History: How did you get permission to film inside schools, particularly in Sioux City [Alex's hometown]?

Hirsch: We had been trying to find schools to film in for quite some time, and we were finding that it was very, very difficult. Most places were highly unreceptive to the idea. It was a great miracle that we connected with the Waitt Institute for Violence Prevention (WIVP) which is based out of Sioux City, and they had invested deeply in the school district there with an anti-bully curriculum, mentoring programs, and gender violence prevention work for probably nearly a decade. It was a perfect storm of having a strong and meaningful introduction to the school district, coupled with a relatively new and progressive superintendent.

We were able to meet the superintendent, present our idea about what we were trying to achieve, and get his buy-in about the value of being able to be inside a school to see what happens, both good and bad. I think that they certainly hoped that it would represent more of the good, but understood that being willing to put themselves out there would be a great value to the nation in a way, to everyone who is trying to do this [respond to bullying], and that they would grow from it and see things that they don't normally see. We were then able to make a presentation before the school board, who took a vote and decided to allow us to come in and film.

We were basically offered carte blanche to a number of schools in the district, and it was left up to us to decide where and how we would focus. . . . We went and shared our vision again with the staff at East Middle School [Alex's school] prior to the start of the school year, and we were also introduced at the first assembly to the students, and we talked to them about what we were doing. So it was a very interesting and a very transparent process. We were given permission to shoot on buses, to shoot inside the principal's office, to be able to capture the full scope of how this stuff works. We also have releases from all of the families of the kids that appear and speak in the film. The families of the bullies in the film all agreed to participate knowing that their child was on film behaving as a bully.

You kept an eye on a lot of stories at once. What criteria did you use to choose which ones to follow more closely?

We were pretty locked into Alex early on. And we were struggling to feel the narrative arc or the urgency in other stories we were following, particularly in the high school. We invested nearly an equal amount of time into filming at the high school in Sioux City, which was a very, very different school. . . . West [High School] had and continues to have really strong and good leadership, and a really strong mentoring program. The difference in culture was like night and day. You could feel it when you walked into the building. You felt it immediately that you were in a different kind of place, where people treated each other better. Ultimately we weren't able to piece together a story out of West, in part because good climate and culture don't manifest themselves as drama. We wanted to really include that world and that culture and what they had achieved there into the film and just ultimately couldn't. When you build a film, you're building blocks that build onto each other narratively; they each have to stand with the one before and the one after it in terms of being relevant, compelling, and meaningful. It was really hard to weave a good normal day into the narrative. Those are some of the things we wrestled with.

I would say that Alex for us was really— for one, we really just fell in love with him and his family. And two, they really let us into their lives. Alex was utterly unaware of the camera. Who he was, in fact his whole family really, they were exactly who they are with the cameras on and with the cameras off. That also matters when you are making a film. You really want to be with someone who is comfortable and open and does let you in that way. All of the families, all the kids, that are in the film, I saw them as partners in telling the story. With each of them, we talked about the meaning of their decision to let us film their struggles and let us into their lives. I was able to share with them my experiences, and why I wanted to make this film, and why I felt their participation was going to make a difference for others. And they universally stepped up to that call and participated for that reason. . . .

It factors back to another universal feeling that I have, which is the kids that are bullied want to have a voice, they want truth, they want to show the world that "this is what I go through and you guys don't listen to me, but it's really bad, it's really, really hard, and I carry this around every day on my own." That is reflected in the ways in which kids write about bullying, they blog about it, think about it, Facebook about it; when there is a local story they write about it, all of those things are reflective of the kind of battling in silence that is part of the landscape.

What was hardest for you to cut from the film?

There were a lot of things that were hard to cut from the film. There was a story that we spent a lot of time on with two families in North Texas. Two boys, Cain and Joe, were both being bullied in the same middle school. We really struggled to put that story in. It fit into a larger story of the fight the parents were having with the school. There had been five suicides within 20 miles of their school. Cain went and spoke to the school board and he clearly articulated the abuse and the things that he went through. You develop strong relationships with your subjects and it's very disappointing to have to ultimately pick up that phone and say, "All those weeks we spent together, all that we shared, unfortunately did not make it into the film." That's very, very difficult.

As a filmmaker, maybe a big part of what you're working up against is simply the amount of time you have to tell the story, which in the face of the story that you are telling doesn't seem like enough.

You are working with time. You are working with how many story lines you can juggle with your audience. How does each story feed into the next? What's the connective fiber? How does David Long saying Tyler had a target on his back link to Alex getting off the school bus and walking home? Those are things with your editing team you really work on because you want your audience to be with you. . . . Also the West High stories were really, really hard to leave out. It was the same kind of phone call: "Hey we filmed in your school for an entire year, but you're not in the movie. Why? Because you were doing things too well." It's a very difficult phone call to make. I can tell you something else, some of those scenes were in play until two weeks before we were finished. . . .

It's hard to leave things out. We had a very robust dialogue when editing a sequence that involved Alex having a really good ride on the bus where he was getting along with all the other kids and laughing. I desperately wanted it in the film and ultimately it was just too confusing. Even in the landscape of bullying, you do have good days and bad days, moments where that's all kind of gone away for a minute and you're just happy and you feel like a normal kid. That's another thing that's difficult to leave out.

In the moments you were filming incidents of bullying, did you ever feel that you should intervene directly to stop the harassment?

It was incredibly difficult not to go and rip those kids off of Alex. Had the violence increased, I'm sure there was a point at which I would have had to, and would have absolutely stopped it. But the reality is that Alex wanted people to know what happens to him. And all of the kids that were in this film wanted people to know what they go through.

A significant part of this journey was and remains the relationship developed between me and the film subjects. The kids and their parents became our partners. Alex and I talked regularly about what was going on in school and what he felt comfortable with having on film. One of the hardest things for a kid who is bullied is to have that evidence to show adults, their parents, and the community what he or she actually endures. The power and strength of having these experiences on film is that they become real and not just testimonial.

Documentary filmmakers generally try not to make themselves part of the story they are documenting. But what we saw on that final bus ride with Alex was so alarming that it became a breaking point for us. Though it was a difficult decision in the moment, we decided to bring evidence of what was happening to the school, Alex's parents, and the Sioux City police department. This absolutely put us into the story and is acknowledged in the film.

Lee Hirsch/The Weinstein Company

Connections

1. Which of Hirsch's comments are most helpful to you in understanding and processing the film? What questions about the film do you still have? The full interview with Hirsch is available at *www.facinghistory.org/safeschools*.

2. Which of the stories that were cut from the film would you most like to learn more about? What would you hope to learn from them?

3. Hirsch comments that, when he walked into Sioux City's West High School, "You felt it immediately that you were in a different kind of place, where people treated each other better."

   How do you account for Hirsch's feeling? What might he have seen or heard that indicated he was in a healthy, respectful environment?

4. How might including footage of "good days" and more positive school environments have changed the impact of the film? If the filmmakers were to make another film about bullying, what types of stories would be most interesting and helpful to you?

Classroom Suggestions

The *Think, Pair, Share* strategy (on page 52) provides students the opportunity to discuss the choices Hirsch made in the film, first in discussion with a partner, and then with the entire class. You can use the Connections questions to begin the conversation.

Notes

1 Lee Hirsch, interview by author, telephone, October 13, 2011.

The Power of Friendship

The presence or absence of friends plays a significant role in the lives of the young people profiled in BULLY. Just as the support of friends lends Kelby perspective on the harassment she endures, the absence of friends is an ongoing source of confusion for Alex. Ty Smalley is missed greatly by his heartbroken and devoted friend Trey.

Psychologist Michael Thompson believes friendships are valuable to young people because they offer companionship, feedback, and support:

> When your children leave your house and disappear into school for the day, they face an array of tasks and an array of opportunities for pleasure, frustration, and pain. In one sense, each child faces these challenges alone. But in another sense they do so in pairs or in groups. Even lonely or isolated children are deeply affected by the status of friendships—or the lack of them. Connecting with a close friend or friends provides them with companions on the journey, allies, cheerleaders, someone to offer feedback to help them figure out just how well, or badly, they're doing at the business of growing up.[1]

As Thompson suggests, friends can have a powerful, positive effect on the lives of those who are bullied. Kelby's friends offer her moments of joy as well as support and affirmation:

> Tyler, Summer, Caitlin, Brooke, if I didn't have them, I wouldn't be here. For sure, like 100%, they are everything that makes me get up and walk in the doors to school every morning. I couldn't do it without them. I've got my, what, four-foot-ten girlfriend to protect me? . . . You know I just keep thinking that maybe I'm the one that is in this town, that can make a change. I don't want them to win, and I don't want to back down, and maybe all it takes is for one person to stand up. You're not just standing up for you. You're standing up for all the kids who go through this, every single day.[2]

Friends also share in the frustration and pain of the bullied, even when they are not harassed themselves. Ty Smalley's friend Trey remembers:

> Ty was just the coolest kid I knew. . . . When people would bully him, I'd get so angry, and I could have hurt those kids so badly that done something to him. Like they'll push him down, and say, 'Shut up spaz,' or throw him into a locker, or shove him into one. And I'd just go to take off after them and he'd be like, 'Trey, it isn't worth it, be better than them, it's all right,' and he'd walk off with a smile. And I don't know how he could do it. He was way stronger than I was. If it was up to me, if I was the king of the United States, I'd make it to where there was no popularity, everyone was equal, because that's how it should be.[3]

For some who are bullied, the need to belong can feel so great that it leads to confusion about who is a friend and who is not. Alex struggles with this question in the following exchange with his mother, after she is shown videotape of him being assaulted on the school bus:

Alex's mom	I would've never guessed in a million years it was that bad. Do you understand that at some point you've gotten used to this? And I'm not, I'm not used to it, because I didn't know, and I'm not about to get used to it. Does it make you feel good when they punch you, or kick you, or stab you? Do these things make you feel good?
Alex	Well, no, well, I don't know. I'm starting to think I don't feel anything anymore.
Alex's mom	I don't understand, Alex. Friends are supposed to make you feel good, that's the point of having them. It's someone else on the planet you can connect with. Your only connection to these kids is that they like to pound on you.
Alex	If you say these people aren't my friends, then what friends do I have?[4]

Classroom Suggestions

The *Big Paper* strategy (page 50) can offer an effective way for students to explore the perspectives in this reading. You can use the quotations from the film in this reading as the basis for this activity. By requiring students to slow down their thinking and communicate only through writing, *Big Paper* gives every student the opportunity to reflect deeply on friendship and to have his or her ideas heard by the class.

Connections

1. What are the characteristics that make someone a good friend? How are good friendships formed? How do you learn to be a good friend to others?

2. How would you respond to Alex's question at the end of his conversation with his mother? What is the difference between a healthy friendship and an unhealthy one? How do young people learn the difference?

3. In her book *Odd Girl Out,* Rachel Simmons writes that girls are more likely than boys to engage in bullying behavior towards friends. She writes, "Unlike boys, who tend to bully acquaintances or strangers, girls frequently attack within tightly knit networks of friends, making aggression harder to identify and intensifying the damage to victims." Simmons also points out that, while boys who bully are more likely to use physical aggression, girls who bully are more likely to use rumors, exclusion, and social manipulation to harm their targets.[5]

   How are friendships between girls different from friendships between boys? Are Simmons's descriptions of the differences in bullying by girls and boys consistent with your experience? Do the stories in BULLY follow these patterns?

4. In the film, Kelby is often interviewed on camera with her friends surrounding her. Trey talks extensively with the filmmakers about losing his friend Ty. In what ways are, or were, Kelby and Ty supported by their friends? What are some ways that you can support a friend who is being bullied?

5. Psychologist Elizabeth Englander suggests that small arguments between adolescents can escalate into incidents of ostracism because with many young people, especially girls, efforts to support friends "can mistakenly translate into feeling that you have to take sides in a conflict."[6] When the majority of a group of friends take the same side in a fight, the remaining few become vulnerable to ostracism and bullying.

   Do you feel obligated to take a friend's side when he or she has a dispute with someone else? In what other ways can you be helpful to a friend who is experiencing a conflict?

6. Psychologist Dennis Barr, a Facing History and Ourselves staff member, writes: "Ideally, friendships offer . . . a base that can help provide a sense of psychological and even physical safety, promoting self-esteem and a sense of belonging."[7] The sense of belonging that friendship offers can help offset the isolation a young person feels when he or she is bullied. Indeed, research on bullying and peer relationships suggests that the effects of being bullied—such as sadness, anxiety, and depression—can be reduced when the child being bullied has a close friend.[8] Educational psychologist Philip Rodkin writes that "even one good friend to a victim of bullying can help assuage the harmful consequences of being harassed."[9]

   How can educators and other adults in the school community help students who struggle with making friends? How might helping students foster healthy friendships reduce the amount of bullying that occurs in a school?

Notes

1 Michael Thompson and Catherine O'Neill Grace, *Best Friends, Worst Enemies: Understanding the Social Lives of Children* (New York: Ballantine Books, 2001), 65.

2 BULLY, directed by Lee Hirsch, 2011.

3 Ibid.

4 Ibid.

5 Rachel Simmons, *Odd Girl Out: The Hidden Culture of Aggression in Girls* (Orlando: Harcourt, Inc., 2002), 3.

6 Elizabeth Englander, interview with Facing History, July 13, 2011.

7 Dennis Barr, "Friendship and Belonging," in *Fostering Friendship: Pair Therapy for Treatment and Prevention,* ed. Robert L. Selman, Caroline L. Watts, and Lynn Hickey Schultz (New York: Aldine de Gruyter, 1997), 26.

8 Philip C. Rodkin, "Bullying and Children's Peer Relationships," in *White House Conference on Bullying Prevention,* 36, accessed October 18, 2011, http://stopbullying.gov/references/white_house_conference/index.html.

9 Rodkin, "Bullying," 35.

Upstanders and Bystanders

Bullying typically involves others besides the tormentor and his or her target. Numerous peers are often aware of the bullying, and they must choose how to respond. The choice comes down to playing one of three roles: perpetrator, bystander, or upstander.

- **Perpetrators** join in the bullying, escalate the harassment, or initiate new attacks on the target later.

- **Bystanders** attempt to remain uninvolved in the situation, often by looking on silently or finding an excuse to walk away.

- **Upstanders** take action to oppose the bullying in some way. They might intervene directly and tell the tormentors to stop, but they need not put themselves at risk in order to be helpful. Upstanders might also respond in other ways such as making friends with the targeted student or seeking help from adults.[1]

These three roles are fluid; everyone can be a perpetrator, bystander, or upstander at different times and in different situations.

Since Ty Smalley's death, his father has devoted himself to inspiring young people to stand up for the victims of bullying. Speaking to a group of teenagers at a Stand for the Silent rally at the end of the film, Kirk Smalley says:

> Go out there and find that one child, that new kid, who just moved to town, standing over there by himself, be his friend, smile, be willing to help him out when he's pushed down, be willing to stand up for him. If we all do it together, we will change the world. It starts right here, right now.[2]

Tyler Long's father, David, is also convinced that upstanders have the potential to make a difference:

> I believe had more kids stepped forward when Tyler was being bullied, and took a stand alongside of Tyler, Tyler would still be here today. Everything starts with one and builds up. And if we can continue to increase the numbers, whether it be one by one, two by two, eventually we have an army, to where we can defeat anything.[3]

There is evidence to back up these fathers' beliefs about the power of upstanders. Research suggests that the reactions of classmates who witness bullying play an important role in affirming or condemning the behavior of the bully.[4] Psychologist Christina Salmivalli writes that when onlookers remain bystanders, "the bully might interpret such behavior as approval of what he or she is doing."[5] But when peers intervene to stop bullying, behaving as upstanders, they are successful *over half the time*. However, witnesses choose to intervene in less than 20% of bullying incidents.[6]

Connections

1. What are the different ways that someone can intervene when he or she witnesses bullying?

   After seeing BULLY as part of a school field trip, one middle school student, Max, posted the following statement on Facebook:

   > I was there today [at the movie screening] and it was very inspiring. After we got back to school we finished our classes, then on the bus a kid was being bullied by some girl. I tried to help him and he was getting very upset after she had been yelling at him and me and a couple of friends talked to him about what we had just saw today and we told him to talk to a counselor and tell her what had happened. If it wasn't for what I saw today I probably would have never stepped in and stopped it to be honest I probably would have just ignored it.[7]

   Was Max an upstander? What did he do to help the boy who was being bullied? What other choices could he have made in this situation?

2. Think about a time when you witnessed bullying. How did you respond? How do you wish you had responded? What stopped you from responding that way?

3. How do you explain why so few bystanders choose to help victims of bullying? What factors make it difficult for peers to act as upstanders when they witness bullying? Is the success rate of upstanders in stopping incidents of bullying surprising to you? Why or why not? Do you think that, if adolescents knew they had more than a 50% chance of making a positive difference, they would be more likely to intervene when they witnessed bullying?

4. Were there any students who were upstanders in the scenarios you viewed in BULLY? If so, how did they make a difference? Were there any students who were bystanders? If so, what could they have done to make a difference?

5. Often offering simple and immediate encouragement to those who have just been bullied can make a big difference. Psychologist Elizabeth Englander points out that victims of bullying consistently tell researchers that this type of upstander behavior is one of the most helpful responses:

> What helped the most was having somebody who came up to them and said, 'Don't listen to him, he talks like that to everyone. There's nothing wrong with you. Why don't you come and eat lunch at my table? Don't worry about that.'[8]

Why do you think that small, simple gestures of kindness can make a big difference to the victims of bullying? What are some other simple actions that peers can take to offer encouragement to those who are bullied?

6. Many researchers have investigated the characteristics and motives of those who bully. Thomas Farmer and Cristin Hall identify two groups of bullies, *those who are socially marginalized* and *those who enjoy high social status*. Both groups participate in bullying because they are "in some way socially vulnerable and use bullying as an expression of power." Socially marginalized bullies are often bullied themselves, and they use this behavior to deflect harassment away from themselves and gain social power. This group is more likely to display poor social skills, and therefore they are also more likely to engage in physical forms of bullying.

High-status bullies, by contrast, typically display strong social skills, and, as a result, they often take on leadership roles in their schools. They are more likely to bully through social aggression: rumors, gossip, ostracism, and defamation of character. According to Farmer and Hall, high-status bullies engage in this behavior as a way to "protect their status and to defend against others who may challenge their social power."[9]

How might understanding the motives of bullies help bystanders and upstanders respond more effectively to the harassment they witness? How might the same factors involving social status make bystanders less willing to intervene?

Classroom Suggestions

The *Attribute Linking* strategy (page 49) enables students to collaborate with a series of partners to consider what it means to be both an upstander and a bystander. By developing their ideas through a series of one-on-one conversations with classmates, students will take into account a variety of perspectives and experiences as they think about the reasons for bystander behavior and the various ways that upstanders can make a difference.

Notes

1 Luba Falk Feigenberg et al., "Belonging to and exclusion from the peer group in schools: Influences on adolescents' moral choices," *Journal of Moral Education* 37, no. 2 (June 2008): 173–74.

2 BULLY, directed by Lee Hirsch, 2011.

3 Ibid.

4 Christina Salmivalli et al., "Bully as a Group Process: Participant Roles and Their Relations to Social Status Within the Group," *Aggressive Behavior* 22 (1996): 2.

5 Christina Salmivalli, "Bullying Is a Group Phenomenon—What Does It Mean And Why Does It Matter?" Education.com: Bullying Reference Center, last modified 2011, accessed November 7, 2011, http://www.education.com/reference/article/peer-social-group-role-in-bullying/.

6 Philip C. Rodkin, "Bullying and Children's Peer Relationships," in *White House Conference on Bullying Prevention*, 36, accessed October 18, 2011, http://stopbullying.gov/references/white_house_conference/index.html.

7 Max S., post to Facebook Web forum, November 16, 2011, http://facebook.com.

8 Elizabeth Englander, interview with Facing History, July 13, 2011.

9 Thomas Farmer and Cristin Hall, "Bullying in School: An Exploration of Peer Group Dynamics," Education.com: Bullying Information Center, last modified 2011, accessed October 31, 2011, http://www.education.com/reference/article/school-bullying-peer-group-dynamics/.

The Impact on Parents

The effects of bullying reach beyond the targeted individuals to their parents. Psychologist Kenneth Rigby reflects on how parents experience and respond to the pain of their children:

> We are apt to think that the hurt and misery of children being bullied at school is experienced solely by the targets or victims and that the solution, at least potentially, lies entirely in the hands of teachers and school counselors. If so, we are mistaken. We forget or fail to acknowledge the deep hurt and misery experienced by the parents of victimized children, their anger, despair and frustration as they learn about how their children are being maliciously treated by their peers and do not know what to do.[1]

In addition to the powerful testimonies of children who experience bullying, the film BULLY also provides a window into the anguish and frustration experienced by parents. Consider the voices of these parents attempting to make sense of their children's predicaments:

Barbara P. (Ja'Meya's mother)

It was about 8:30 to 8:45 when I got the call, that morning. I was shocked, because I couldn't believe that was my daughter. And I asked the lady, 'Are you sure you got my daughter?' And she said, 'Yeah.' And I said, 'Well what is her name.' And she said, 'Ja'Meya Jackson.' And it's like I just, my heart dropped. 'Cause I couldn't believe it. I'm like, 'She couldn't have gotten my gun.' And she said, 'She got your gun.' And I'm like, 'She didn't hurt anybody did she?' She said, 'No, she didn't hurt anybody.'

Sheriff Tommy Vaughn

Even though things came out as best as they possibly could have, if you added up all the years that she could get, it'd be hundreds of years.

Barbara P.

Yeah, that would devastate me, I don't even know if I could live behind that. I really don't.

Jackie L. (Alex's mother)

Kinda sucks that it's Mother's Day, I haven't felt like a very good mother today. Alex, he just can't fit in, he tries. He just comes across too weird to people, you know. But what really ticks me off, is if they got to know him, he'd probably be the most devoted friend they ever had.

Kirk Smalley (Ty's father)

You know, we're nobodies. I guarantee you, if some politician's kid did this, because he was getting picked on at a public school, there'd be a law tomorrow, there'd be changes made tomorrow. We're nobody, but we love each other and we loved our son.

David Long (Tyler's father)

If there is a heaven, I know Tyler's there. And all I can do is have the faith that I'll be able to see him again. That's what I have to live for. And I have to live for my other two kids and I have to make their life as comfortable and as pleasant and as peaceful as I can. Tyler Lee Long, born April 25, 1992, died October 17, 2009, age 17.

Bob J. (Kelby's father)

I never knew, the saying you don't know what a person's been through until you walk a mile in their shoes, I never understood the depth of that meaning until I had a gay child. It has made me completely reevaluate who and what I am as a human being to see the ugliness that has come out.[2]

Classroom Suggestions

Big Paper, Think, Pair, Share, and *Save the Last Word for Me* (on pages 50, 52, and 54) are all strategies that you might use with this reading to facilitate in-depth, thoughtful discussion about what parents experience when their children are bullied. Connections 4 and 5 may provide a compelling focus for your discussion with students.

If you are working with a group that includes both students and parents, consider using the *Fishbowl* strategy (on page 46). That way, students and parents could take turns discussing the reading while the others listen silently.

Connections

1. How do the voices of these parents, and those of other parents in the film, deepen our understanding of the destructive impact of bullying?

2. Psychologist Richard Weissbourd comments, "Parents have complicated responses [when their children are bullied]. . . . They may have experienced bullying themselves, feel shame that their children are experiencing it, and feel helpless too." For parents, Weissbourd continues, "it is key to build some self-awareness about their own complicated feelings."[3] How might parents' own experiences of bullying—as bully, victim, or bystander—affect the way that they respond when their children are bullied? How might parents draw on their own experiences in order to be more helpful to their children? How might parents' experiences of bullying make it more difficult for them to help?

3. How might telling the stories of their sons' experiences help the Longs and Smalleys heal? How might their experiences as parents of children who committed suicide make them effective advocates for the victims of bullying?

4. Many of the victims of bullying in this film talk openly and candidly about their experiences to the filmmakers. How do you account for the fact that Alex, for instance, is able to share his experiences with the filmmakers but has such a hard time talking about it with his parents? In what ways is Alex's reluctance to communicate with his parents typical for adolescents?

5. Alex's parents acknowledge the difficulty of communicating with him about his torment on the bus. At one point, his mother tells his father, "Probably the only thing worse than being bullied all day is to have to come home and tell you."[4] They better understand the severity of what Alex is enduring when the filmmakers show them footage of the abuse. How can parents know when their children are being bullied? What are the barriers that keep parents from knowing and understanding?

6. Researchers Danah Boyd and Alice Marwick point to the language that teenagers use to describe bullying and other conflicts at school as one reason that parents are often left in the dark. According to their studies, teenagers use the vague term "drama" to deflect concerns about bullying:

   > Dismissing a conflict that's really hurting their feelings as drama lets teenagers demonstrate that they don't care about such petty concerns. They can save face while feeling superior to those tormenting them by dismissing them as desperate for attention. . . . Teenagers want to see themselves as in control of their own lives; their reputations are important. Admitting that they're being bullied, or worse, that they are bullies, slots them into a narrative that's disempowering and makes them feel weak and childish.[5]

   How can young people and their parents set the stage for better communication? Do parents need to listen more carefully, or do their children need to communicate more clearly? Or do parents and children need to work together to create an environment in which sharing is welcome? What steps can they take?

Notes

1 Kenneth Rigby, "Children, Parents and School Bullying," Education.com: Bullying Information Center, last modified 2011, accessed October 27, 2011, http://www.education.com/reference/article/bullying-effect-on-home-life/.

2 BULLY, directed by Lee Hirsch, 2011.

3 Richard Weissbourd, interview by author, telephone, November 4, 2011.

4 BULLY, directed by Lee Hirsch, 2011.

5 Danah Boyd and Alice Marwick, "Bullying as True Drama," editorial, *The New York Times*, September 22, 2011, accessed October 27, 2011, http://www.nytimes.com/2011/09/23/opinion/why-cyberbullying-rhetoric-misses-the-mark.html.

Adult Intervention

Parents are not the only adults who struggle to find out what is going on in the social lives of children. Most bullying occurs out of sight of teachers and school administrators as well. Often the first step to intervening is for adults to try to determine exactly what is happening, but the truth can be elusive. Students who bully are unlikely to admit the torment they cause. Bystanders, for a variety of reasons, including fear of being bullied themselves, are often reticent to turn in the tormenters.[1] Also, children who are bullied often do not want to admit to their vulnerability and inability to make the harassment stop.[2] Finally, victims of bullying often think that adults will make the situation worse.

As a result, when adults attempt to intervene in bullying and other social conflicts, they often find themselves acting with an incomplete understanding of the situation. BULLY includes some powerful examples of this dynamic as it unfolds. Consider the efforts of Kim Lockwood, an assistant principal in Sioux City, to mediate a conflict between two boys as they come in from recess:

Kim Lockwood	Cole, you stay right here. Right here. I'm going to ask you guys to shake hands. Can you do that?
Glen	Yeah.
Kim Lockwood	Cole! Cole, you are not going anywhere. He is offering his hand and let this drop.
Cole	Ohhh. [Refuses to shake hands.]
Kim Lockwood	[To Glen] You may go. Cole, I expected more.
Cole	He criticizes me every single day.
Kim Lockwood	Then why are you around him?
Cole	I don't, he comes to me. I try to get away, he follows me. And then he criticizes me calling me a p-u-s-s-y.
Kim Lockwood	Okay, honey, that's not right, and he shouldn't do that.
Cole	I don't even know why.
Kim Lockwood	But you know what, he was trying to say he was sorry.
Cole	He already did and he didn't mean it because it continued on.
Kim Lockwood	You didn't mean it when you stuck out your hand either. So that means you're just like him, right, what you don't like in him, you —
Cole	Except I don't hurt people.
Kim Lockwood	By not shaking his hand, you're just like him.
Cole	Like someone who punches you into walls, threatens to break your arm, threatens to stab you and kill you.
Kim Lockwood	Okay.
Cole	Shoot you with a gun?
Kim Lockwood	He a—, he apologized. And have you reported all that sort of stuff?
Cole	Yes.
Kim Lockwood	Okay, then it's been taken care of.
Cole	And all of them said, even the cops told him to stay away from me, and he doesn't.
Kim Lockwood	Okay, can you try and get along? I think you guys might be really good friends at some time.
Cole	We were. And then he started bullying me.[2]

Paula Crandall, another assistant principal in the same school, takes a more methodical approach when responding to the latest incidents of intense bullying Alex endures on the school bus. She interviews several students from the bus separately, and she issues consequences and warnings to several of them. Yet, when talking to Alex, she learns that he is not confident that her response will make a difference:

Paula Crandall	What's one thing that you need to start doing that you haven't done?
Alex H.	Tell someone.
Beverly Bass	Yes.
Paula Crandall	Do you trust us that we'll do something when you tell us that someone's bothering you?
Alex H.	Well, in 6th grade you, uh, did nothing about, uh, Teddy sitting on my head.
Beverly Bass	On the bus?
Alex H.	Yeah, there's like a little knob, then once you unlock that knob you can lift up the seat. And he lifted up the seat, put my head in it, sat on my head.
Paula Crandall	How do you know we didn't do anything?
Alex H.	I don't know, 'cause . . .
Paula Crandall	Alex, did he sit on your head after you told me? I did talk to him and he didn't do that again did he?
Alex H.	No, but he was still doing other stuff after that.[3]

Lee Hirsch/The Weinstein Company

Connections

1. What do you notice about the way Kim Lockwood and Paula Crandall responded to these incidents of bullying? How could they have responded more helpfully to the harassment that Cole and Alex reported to them? How would you like school officials to respond in these type of situations? Why is it so difficult for the school officials to keep the two boys safe?

2. Adults often make sincere efforts to stop bullying behavior in their schools, but in their rush to respond to specific incidents they can forget to listen empathically to the students who are bullied. Psychologist Stephanie Jones comments on the need to listen: "Kids definitely want strategies. They want to know, 'What can I do tomorrow?' But it is essential for adults first to listen and understand deeply, then have strategies develop out of that understanding."[4]

Anna Nolin, the principal of a middle school in Massachusetts, acknowledges that educators often do not feel prepared to respond effectively to bullying, but she urges them to be careful listeners:

> You don't need counseling training to sit and hear the story and really listen for what is getting at this student, and have a tolerance for the fact that that story may change and evolve over the telling because the student is coming to understand their own perspective.[5]

What are some of the challenges that teachers, administrators, and school staff members face in their efforts to learn the truth about instances of bullying and ensure safety and fairness for all students? What factors might leave students feeling like the adults did not listen carefully and understand their perspective?

3. In many schools, adults can and do respond to bullying in helpful ways. Discussing a specific example of ostracism among middle school girls (see the Ostracism Case Study in this guide on pages 41–44), Nolin outlines how her school would make careful listening a key part of their response:

> I would've begun with using my administrative team to interview the girls and get their . . . very nuanced and detailed perspective. Then I would gather the adults around that would be in charge of dealing with these students—so that would be the guidance counselor, psychologist, their grade level administrator—and we would do an

analysis of the different girls' stories and try to come to an understanding of the girls' perspectives. We may have to revisit that with them, but we would continuously try to refine our understanding of the girls' perspectives.[6]

What do you notice about Nolin's response to an incident of ostracism? What is her goal? What additional actions do educators need to take to address these situations effectively?

4. Researchers Philip Rodkin and Ramin Karimpour write that some bullies are "hidden in plain sight." This can be the case when the student who bullies others is well-connected and socially prominent in a school, and therefore less likely to be perceived as having a negative impact on other students.[7] Similarly, Lee Hirsch asks, "How prized are some bullies to the community?" He wonders if some students who are considered important to the school community, such as star athletes or academic leaders, get the benefit of the doubt from adults when they are involved in bullying others.[8]

How might adults' biases and beliefs about specific students affect their responses to bullying behavior? How can they avoid developing such blind spots that affect their ability to respond effectively?

5. While bullying often happens out of view of adults, that is not always the case. After viewing the film, psychologist Richard Weissbourd stated, "If you are not a parent or teacher, you still have a responsibility to intervene in bullying."[9]

Alex's mother wonders about the adult supervision on her son's school bus:

> When I was on the bus when I was a kid, if you got out of your seat, they pulled over, the whole world stopped until everybody sat down and shut up. How come they don't do anything now, they just drive? There should be more responsibility than that.[10]

What factors might prevent a school bus driver from stopping bullying and other forms of harassment on the bus? What are some strategies schools might implement to ensure students' safety from harassment on school buses?

What is the impact of an adult witnessing bullying and choosing not to intervene? What messages does adult inaction send to the bullies, victims, and bystanders? How is the impact of an adult bystander different from that of a peer bystander?

In the process of making BULLY, the filmmakers witnessed a significant amount of bullying. Eventually they intervened by showing footage of Alex being assaulted to his parents, the school, and the police. To what extent did the filmmakers have a responsibility to stop the bullying they witnessed?

6. Lee Hirsch believes that educators need to address bullying more proactively in their schools. The first step, he says, is simply to observe more carefully:

> I would argue that someone that was looking with a keen eye, looking to understand and to see, could walk into a lunchroom and within five minutes point out the kids in that lunchroom that were bullied. That's an important thing. If that is the case, then that means there is a case to be made to look harder and track those kids and be aware of those kids and understand what might be weighing on the shoulders of a particular student over time and in many cases over years.[11]

If educators were to observe the lunch room in the manner that Hirsch suggests, what might they look for? How can they determine which students are being bullied or who might be at risk? And, using their observations, how might educators then effectively confirm their theories and protect these students?

7. The emergence of cyberbullying has added significant complexity to the ability of adults to respond. Cyberbullying generally occurs in public, online spaces that can be made visible to anyone, but that does not mean that instances of cyberbullying are easy to find or monitor in the vast landscape of cyberspace. Adults often lack the tools, and sometimes the knowledge of technology, to know where to look. Even if a victim or witness of cyberbullying shows an adult the harassing messages that have been posted online, the identity of the bully can easily be obscured and the number of peers who saw the posts can be difficult to determine.[12]

Who is responsible for dealing with bullying that occurs online? What specific responsibilities do schools, parents, and peers have?

Is it enough to react to incidents of cyberbullying? What can school communities do to prevent cyberbullying proactively?

Notes

1   Ken Rigby and Bruce Johnson, "Innocent Bystanders?" *Teacher,* September 2004, 39–40, accessed October 28, 2011, http://www.kenrigby.net/Innocent-bystanders.pdf.

2   BULLY, directed by Lee Hirsch, 2011.

3   Ibid.

4   Stephanie Jones, interview by author, telephone, November 4, 2011.

5   "Anna Nolin on the Role of the Teacher," Bullying: A Case Study in Ostracism, last modified 2011, accessed November 8, 2011, http://ostracism.facinghistory.org/video/anna-nolin-teacher.

6   "Anna Nolin on What Schools Can Do," Bullying: A Case Study in Ostracism, last modified 2011, accessed November 8, 2011, http://ostracism.facinghistory.org/video/anna-nolin-what-schools-can-do.

7   Philip C. Rodkin, "Bullying and Children's Peer Relationships," in *White House Conference on Bullying Prevention,* 36, accessed October 18, 2011, http://stopbullying.gov/references/white_house_conference/index.html.

8   Lee Hirsch, interview by author, telephone, October 13, 2011.

9   Richard Weissbourd, interview by author, telephone, November 4, 2011.

10 BULLY, directed by Lee Hirsch, 2011.

11 Lee Hirsch, interview by author, telephone, October 13, 2011.

12 Sameer Hinduja and Justin W. Patchin, "Overview of Cyberbullying," in *White House Conference on Bullying Prevention,* 21–23, accessed October 28, 2011, http://stopbullying.gov/references/white_house_conference/index.html.

Nurturing School Culture

Each instance of bullying takes place within a larger social context, comprised of the relationships among students, teachers, administrators, and staff of the school, as well as the members of the community and larger society in which that school resides. The relationships among all of these people contribute to the culture of the school. Researchers have found that the quality of a school's culture makes a tremendous difference in the amount of bullying that takes place there.

Director Lee Hirsch concludes that preventing bullying requires that we do more than institute anti-bullying policies and punish bullies. "Combating bullying effectively is not about zero-tolerance policies but about changing hearts and minds," he says. Hirsch hopes his film will inspire this change.

> The power of BULLY is in the experience of what people go through [watching it]. And when they see these stories, they mirror their own experiences, they mirror their own memories, they mirror things that they stood by and witnessed and didn't intervene in, or participated in, or were a victim of, because everybody ultimately has a place in the story.[1]

In other words, to combat bullying effectively, all of the members of the community must work together to change a school's culture. By doing so, communities can address the problem of bullying proactively, rather than only reacting when it occurs.

The complexity of the community and culture surrounding a school is illustrated in BULLY in the aftermath of Tyler Long's suicide in Murray County, Georgia. Five weeks after his death, Tyler's parents organized a town hall meeting to bring their community together to talk about bullying. Several of the viewpoints expressed by town members at this meeting are represented in the following transcript from the film:

Tina Long

My name's Tina Long, I'm Tyler's mother, um, I'm a nurse, and I appreciate y'all being here.

David Long

I'm David Long. And I too really wanted to thank everybody for coming out tonight and being here.

David Carroll (moderator)

We have invited either superintendent or anyone from central office or school board members to participate. So I want to say right up front, if anyone's here from Murray County schools, we'd love to have you up here to represent the school system. . . . Okay, we did invite them, I wish someone had come, uh, that's all you can do.

Jeff Johnson

My name's Jeff Johnson, I run a business here, I'm also a pastor at a local church, some of the church kids came to me after Tyler had committed this awful thing and they said that kids came to school on the next school day with ropes around their neck. And my question to the school board would be, why, in god's name, would some teacher, some counselor, somebody in enforcement not do something, because that is very derogatory to any kid. That's like a slap in the face to these parents. And my question is, if bartenders are responsible for a drunk that goes out and kills an innocent person, how come the bullies are not responsible for the death of this precious child?

State Representative
This is an awfully complicated and difficult issue. I know there's a lot of anger about the school system here. But the school can't by itself change a child's behavior if they're going home and, and not being reinforced at home to change their behavior.

Nurse
Good luck with that. Most of these parents, I hate to say it, could care less. We've been there, done that, you're not going to get them in there, so then what do you do? Um, we've been in this scenario, and um, you couldn't get the parents involved. So then what do you do? And we went to the police. Their hands are tied. You go to the school, um, kids will be kids. Let these girls work it out. Let your child work it out. Well, it's not just in school. They go on the Internet, cell phones. They can damage somebody's life, like they did your son.

Howard Ensley
Yes, I'm Howard Ensley, I'm the sheriff here in Murray County. We have school resource officers in the school and they're there to protect the students.

Tina Long
Mr. Ensley, last year, when two children beat Tyler up, your school resource officer refused to file the charges. I had to fight. Here what we get is, there's nothing wrong, we didn't do anything, everything's fine. But bottom line here is, when you send your child to that school, doesn't matter what parents that child has, they should be safe and protected. Period.

David Carroll (moderator)
There's a young man back there with his hand up. Are you a student? Okay, if you would.

Boy
Um, I was a very good friend of Tyler Long's, and whenever you would walk around that school, you notice that everybody gets bullied. And then the teachers just kind of shrug it off. As in, oh, he done something wrong to that kid, that's why he got what he got. And it's okay, it's just fine. That's a load of daggom crap. It's a big lie.

David Carroll (moderator)
All right DJ, thank you very much.

Devon M.
I've been dealing with it for the, for four years. And I finally got tired of it.

David Carroll (moderator)
So one day you had enough, what'd you do?

Devon M.
I just went off on the kid, because I couldn't stand it anymore, I couldn't take it. It came to the point that last year I stayed out of school purposefully to try to stay away from them, I've been to my mom, my parents, and the principal all for the last three years, and they haven't done anything about it. It's a shame that Tyler had to do what he done for people to notice what's going on in the schools in Murray County. It's a shame that he had to do this for anybody to notice it.

David Long
We can make a difference, we can make a difference so kids don't have to go through four years of torment and sadness and not wanting to go to school. As I told the school board, my voice is not going to fall silent. I will go to my grave until a difference is made.

Devon M.
I know what Tyler was going through. I know how he was thinking about suicide. They went around, they were calling me a pussy, shoving me into lockers, saying, "F you," and now, after I've actually stood up for myself, they just walk by me like oh, there's another kid. It's just another kid here at our school. It really came down to the point that I had to go myself and literally stand up for myself for them to leave me alone.[2]

Connections

1. Is there a word or phrase from one of the participants in the town hall meeting that stands out to you? Why? Which contributions from the town hall meeting resonate most with you and your experience as a student, educator, or parent?

2. Twenty administrators from the Murray County school system were invited to the town meeting, but none attended. What might be some reasons that school officials chose not to attend?

   David Carroll, the local television news reporter who moderated the meeting, later wrote that, if the school administrators had attended,

   > they would have heard students tearfully detailing being bullied, wrongly accused, and humiliated in open-stall bathrooms. They would have heard constructive suggestions for more, better trained resource officers. Ideas on student honor councils to better enforce and encourage good behavior. Plans to establish parent advocate groups to help families approach school officials on bullying issues. Goals of uniting churches and support groups to educate families on spotting both bullies and victims. And heart-tugging testimony from Tyler Long's younger siblings, 15-year-old twins Taryn and Troy, who have endured bullying and ridicule themselves, even after Tyler's death.[3]

   What do the contributions from those who did attend tell you about the community there?

3. If such a forum on bullying were held in your community, who do you think would attend? What might the participants say about the culture of your school and community?

4. What does Hirsch mean when he says that "everyone has a place in the story"? What has been your role with regards to bullying or its prevention in your community? What role would you like to play in the future?

5. The town hall meeting was emotional, even painful, for many of the attendees. To what extent are difficult discussions about bullying an important part of addressing the problem? How do we engage in conversations about bullying that are often uncomfortable and emotional without making some school officials, parents, and students defensive?

6. Psychologist Philip Rodkin asserts, "Classroom and school climates are built by the relationships peers have to one another and to their teachers. These interpersonal bonds need to be healthy, or bullying and antisocial behavior can overpower the learning environment." He goes on to suggest that teachers take the time periodically to ask their students directly about their social relationships in general and bullying in particular.[4]

   What are the implications of Rodkin's thinking on the roles of educators? What are the responsibilities of teachers beyond providing instruction in the subjects they teach? How might teachers integrate care and concern for the relationships between students and teachers into their classroom instruction, regardless of the subject they teach?

7. Research suggests that bullying behaviors are more prevalent in schools with autocratic, hierarchical cultures than in schools with democratic, egalitarian cultures.[5] Do you agree? How would you characterize the culture in your school? What do you think needs to change? How does a school community go about making its culture more democratic?

8. Thabiti Brown, principal of a public charter high school in Dorchester, Massachusetts, places a priority on proactively nurturing his school's culture in order to prevent bullying:

[T]he issue of striving for social justice—we value that. Being careful and thoughtful and a caring member of your community—we value that. So how much do you put into that? . . . [W]e invest heavily in these resources that are meant to get students . . . to look at each other as human beings and support each other.[6]

What priorities compete with nurturing a healthy culture in your school? What strategies can schools use to ensure that focus on school culture is maintained?

Brown says that part of building a positive school culture is focusing on the little things. Any exchange between members of the school community, no matter how brief or insignificant, that is not imbued with respect can lead to a much more harmful situation. What are some of the little things that occur at your school that either help or hurt the school culture?

9. Creating social norms (accepted standards of behavior within a community) that promote respect is key to improving school culture, according to Alan Heisterkamp, an educational consultant who has worked extensively with the schools in Sioux City. By discussing and practicing with students "real-life" ways to intervene in bullying and other forms of abusive behavior, Heisterkamp believes that schools can encourage upstander behavior. "As a young person, the more I think other peers are likely to intervene, the more likely I am to intervene," explains Heisterkamp.[7]

Do the social norms in your school community encourage students to be upstanders? What steps can a community take to change its accepted standards of behavior? What kind of commitment is necessary to make this happen?

10. What strategies does your school use to address bullying? Which strategies are most effective? Which are least effective? What do you do in your school to help combat bullying? What do you need to know more about in order to respond to or prevent bullying more effectively? In what areas do you need more support from your peers, teachers, parents, or administrators?

Notes

1 Lee Hirsch, interview by author, telephone, October 13, 2011.

2 BULLY, directed by Lee Hirsch, 2011.

3 David Carroll, "COMMENTARY: David Carroll on Murray County Bullying Forum," WRCBtv.com, last modified December 4, 2009, accessed October 28, 2011, http://www.wrcbtv.com/Global/story.asp?S=11604070.

4 Philip C. Rodkin, "Bullying and Children's Peer Relationships," in White House Conference on Bullying Prevention, 37–38, accessed October 18, 2011, http://stopbullying.gov/references/white_house_conference/index.html.

5 Rodkin, "Bullying," 36–37.

6 "Thabiti Brown on Building a Positive School Climate," Bullying: A Case Study in Ostracism, last modified 2011, accessed November 8, 2011, http://ostracism.facinghistory.org/video/thabiti-brown-climate.

7 Alan Heisterkamp, "RE: Bully Project 1st draft," E-mail message to Karen Barss, November 21, 2011.

CONTINUING THE CONVERSATION

This section provides an effective way to extend the work around bullying that your class or community started after viewing BULLY. The activities and materials included here are not intended to be used immediately after viewing the film. Rather, they are intended to help you continue to facilitate, throughout the school year, the deep reflection and important conversations that the film inspires and the topic of bullying requires.

These materials are centered on a real-life incident of ostracism that took place in a middle school classroom. The story was documented as part of research conducted by Harvard University and Facing History and Ourselves, funded by the Carnegie Corporation of New York, on improving intergroup relations among youth. While this story is different in many ways from those in the film, the themes are similar: the experience of being bullied or ostracized, the meaning of friendship, the impact of upstanders and bystanders, the role of adults, and the power of school culture.

Lee Hirsch/The Weinstein Company

The two readings that follow were adapted from *Bullying: A Case Study in Ostracism,* a Facing History and Ourselves digital resource that explores this story in more depth. The entire resource—including additional suggestions for implementation, commentary from experts, and an online discussion forum—is available at *http://ostracism.facinghistory.org/.* We encourage you to explore the full version online and use it with your classroom or community if you would like to offer a more robust activity.

This abridged version is more suitable for provoking meaningful discussion within a shorter period of time, such as a single class period. The first reading includes a summary of the story. The second includes quotations from several of the students involved, as well as their teacher. Both pages include Connections questions for reflection and discussion.

Scene from a Middle School Classroom: Summary

The Setting: The public school where this incident took place is located in a suburb bordering upon a major city. Families living in the neighborhood surrounding the school range from working class to affluent, and a small percentage of students are bused to the school from the city as part of a long-standing desegregation program.

The Story: *The following description of the incident is based on interviews with the students and teachers involved.*

In December of seventh grade in a public school, Sue and Rhonda considered each other best friends. They belonged to a popular group of girls, including Jill, Patty, Tina, and others. All of these girls had known one another for most of elementary school, except for Tina, who had just moved to the school.

One day, Sue wrote a note to Rhonda saying that she thought their friend Jill was "stupid to break up with her boyfriend." Also in the note, Sue asked Rhonda to keep the note private because she had not yet told Jill herself that she felt that way about her breakup. Rhonda told Jill what Sue had written anyway. When Jill found out about Sue's note, she confronted Sue after school, and they argued in front of many peers. School staff heard the argument and broke it up. Although the argument was brief, the fight snowballed, resulting in many students joining together against Sue. Rhonda and Tina sided with Jill, and they influenced other girls to do the same.

For the rest of seventh grade and almost all of eighth grade, these girls excluded Sue from her former group of friends, teased her and put her down, avoided and ignored her, spread rumors about her, wrote hurtful letters, and made prank telephone calls to her home. Other students, including some boys who were not originally involved, joined in. Most students, if they did not participate directly, kept Sue at a distance and did not stand up for her. Lorna, a girl who had not been a member of this popular group when the ostracism began, was one of the few students who tried to help Sue feel welcome within her group of friends. Nevertheless, Sue went from being a very strong student to getting poor grades and not wanting to go to school.

When adults became aware of the situation, they tried to help. School administrators and a guidance counselor had many conversations with each of the girls and their parents. Some teachers addressed the ostracism directly or indirectly in their teaching. Peer mediators and their advisor from a local high school were invited to help the girls resolve the situation. None of these strategies, however, significantly improved the situation, and some students felt the adults' involvement made things worse.

The ostracism continued when the students returned to school in the fall of eighth grade. Ms. Smith, their eighth grade language arts teacher, was well aware of what had been happening among the students. She gave much thought to the issues raised by Sue's exclusion and how she could touch on the idea of friendship, peer groups, power, and responsibility through what she taught.

Sue and Rhonda both told us that their relationship had improved by the end of eighth grade, although neither of them appeared to have much awareness about how things had improved.

Connections

1. Is this story familiar? What elements of the story feel most familiar?

2. What choices did Rhonda have after she received the note from Sue? Did she do the right thing by telling Jill?

3. Once Rhonda shared Sue's note with Jill, what choices did Jill have about how to react?

4. What might have motivated Sue to write the note about Jill in the first place? What could Sue have done after Jill found out about the note? Why did the other students get involved?

5. Why was Sue ostracized? How is her experience similar to those who were bullied in BULLY? How is her experience different?

6. What effect did the conflict that began with Sue, Jill, and Rhonda have on other students in the class?

7. Why do you think this event turned out this way? How can you explain the actions of the girls and boys in this situation?

8. What would you want to ask each of the students in this case study if you had the opportunity to interview them?

9. What was the role of teachers, parents, and other adults in responding to this incident? What kind of intervention by adults would be most helpful?

10. How is ostracism similar to other forms of bullying? How is it different?

11. Why is ostracism such a powerful weapon? Why is it so painful to be ostracized?

Scene from a Middle School Classroom: Points of View

Patty, a white girl from a middle-class family, did not see herself as a leader among her friends.

It's sort of weird, 'cause you'd never expect somebody who was as popular as she was to, like, be sort of like, shunned from the group by everyone else, but we sort of like we all just went against her. She talked about people behind their back . . . but I think other people did that, too. . . . I really don't know . . . why we were so willing to jump on her and attack her more than anyone else.

It sort of seemed like it was a cool thing to do . . . to be mean to her. And I guess it felt good to be able to get your anger out on a person regardless of whether or not they really deserved to be the person. . . . It sort of seemed like sort of exciting, like it was something you could talk about.

There's a lot of pressure to act a certain way, to be a certain way. . . . You're like afraid to say things. . . .

It seemed like when one or two people decided they didn't like her, then everybody else was like, "OK, we don't like her either," regardless. And I think a lot of people didn't have reasons to dislike her. They just wanted to do it because their friends were doing it.

Rhonda, an African American girl from an urban, working-class family, saw herself as a leader among her friends.

[Sue] wrote me a letter saying that Jill was ignorant to break up with [her boyfriend]. And so, I showed Jill that, and Jill got mad. And then Sue got mad at me because she said in the letter don't show this to anybody, but I showed it anyway, 'cause I felt obligated to show it to her because it wasn't, like, right for Sue to do something like that. Then we all got mad at each other.

The groups changed significantly. There was more people on our side than on Sue's side, but the teachers was on Sue's side. So then it seemed like teachers were, like, the teachers together would probably be more than as many kids as was on our side. So that the teachers had more, they have more power than us. . . .

Sue, an Asian American girl from a working-class family, was a leader among her friends until her argument with Jill.

I think the fact that I am Asian has a lot, actually, to do with it. Not why I was being picked on, it was more to do with why the fight got as big as it did. I think, I mean, because I was a minority it was easier for them to pick on me.

Lorna, an African American student from an urban, working-class family, was not close friends with the other girls in the case study.

I saw something happen to another girl in the school that I didn't really approve of. I have an idea of who was doing it . . . [but I did not try to stop them]. I didn't really know her, so I, like, kind of stayed away from her. . . . I just wasn't a part of it.

Jill, a white girl from an upper middle-class family, did not see herself as having much influence on others.

I know it had a lot to do with me, and there was a lot of teasing that went on that I was involved with, and I don't think that was right. She [Sue] was put out, outcasted, and I don't think that was right at all. And I know I was teasing her . . . to fit in, but I also did not feel comfortable saying, "Oh, I'm not going to tease her."

Mrs. Smith, the girls' language arts teacher as the conflict unfolded, was aware of the conflict, but she was unsure how to help.

[I]t eventually involved teacher intervention. Not myself, I mean, I was concerned about it, but it was really something that the counselor really had a part in, and the principal and some parents were called in, and even then it wasn't resolved because some kids just couldn't see it. They just couldn't see that this was, you know, something that teachers should be involved in, or parents should be involved in. Some parents thought it was silly and foolish that, you know. . . . It was really an interesting situation, and yet, one girl was tremendously hurt by it.

Connections

1. Which comments stand out to you? Why? Which comments ring most true? How?

2. If you were an adult in each of the student's lives (e.g., teacher, parent), what would you want each to consider that was not apparent in their comments on the incident? What if you were one of their peers?

3. Select one quotation from these two pages that especially interests you. Take a few minutes to write about how you would respond to the student who made that remark. What would you want to say to that student? In what ways can you identify with her words?

4. Did any students act as upstanders in this situation? How might the outcome have been different if more students acted as upstanders? What might an upstander do in this situation to improve the outcome?

DISCUSSION STRATEGIES

This section provides descriptions of a variety of strategies and activities that Facing History and Ourselves has found effective in facilitating meaningful discussion about sensitive topics. The primary goal of all of these strategies is to provide a structure for group discussion and analysis that enables every voice to be heard and encourages active listening by all members of the group. After all, the research on bullying tells us that it is in just these types of environments that bullying is least likely to take hold.

The descriptions of these strategies are written for teachers to use with students, but it is our experience that these strategies are effective with groups of adults as well. The Classroom Suggestions that follow many readings in previous sections of this guide reference specific strategies from this section. Please keep in mind that these are only suggestions. We encourage teachers and facilitators to browse through this section, familiarize themselves with many of the strategies included, and use their best judgment to determine which are best suited for their groups.

Lee Hirsch/The Weinstein Company

The following strategies and activities are included in this section:

- **Fishbowl** (p. 46)
- **Identity Chart** (p. 48)
- **Attribute Linking** (p. 49)
- **Big Paper** (p. 50)
- **Think, Pair, Share** (p. 52)
- **Improving the Script** (p. 53)
- **Save the Last Word for Me** (p. 54)

Fishbowl

Rationale

Fishbowl is a teaching strategy that helps students practice being contributors and listeners in a discussion. Students ask questions, present opinions, and share information when they sit in the "fishbowl" circle, while students on the outside of the circle listen carefully to the ideas presented and pay attention to process. Then the roles reverse. This strategy is especially useful when you want to make sure all students participate in the discussion, when you want to help students reflect on what a "good discussion" looks like, and when you need a structure for discussing controversial or difficult topics.

Procedure

1. Selecting a topic for the fishbowl
Almost any topic is suitable for a fishbowl discussion. The most effective prompts (question or text) do not have one right answer, but rather allow for multiple perspectives and opinions. The fishbowl is an excellent strategy to use when discussing dilemmas, for example.

2. Setting up the room
A fishbowl requires a circle of chairs (the "fishbowl") and enough room around the circle for the remaining students to observe what is happening in the fishbowl. Sometimes teachers place enough chairs for half of the students in the class to sit in the fishbowl, while other times teachers limit the chairs in the fishbowl. Typically six to twelve chairs allows for a range of perspectives while still allowing each student an opportunity to speak. The observing students often stand around the fishbowl.

3. Preparation
Like many structured conversations, fishbowl discussions are most effective when students have had a few minutes to prepare ideas and questions in advance.

4. Discussing norms and rules of the discussion
There are many ways to structure a fishbowl discussion. Sometimes teachers have half the class sit in the fishbowl for 10–15 minutes and then say, "Switch," at which point the listeners enter the fishbowl and the speakers become the audience. Another common fishbowl format is the "tap" system, where students on the outside of the fishbowl gently tap a student on the inside, indicating that they should switch roles. See the Variations section for more ideas about how to structure this activity.

Regardless of the particular rules you establish, you want to make sure these are explained to students beforehand. You also want to provide instructions for the students in the audience. What should they be listening for? Should they be taking notes? Before beginning the fishbowl, you may wish to review guidelines for having a respectful conversation. Sometimes teachers ask audience members to pay attention to how these norms are followed by recording specific aspects of the discussion process such as the number of interruptions, respectful or disrespectful language used, or speaking times (who is speaking the most? the least?).

5. Debriefing the fishbowl discussion
After the discussion, you can ask students to reflect on how they think the discussion went and what they learned from it. Students can also evaluate their participation as listeners and as participants. They could also provide suggestions for how to improve the quality of discussion in the future. These reflections can be in writing, or can be structured as a small or large group conversation.

Variations

A fishbowl for opposing positions

This is a type of group discussion that can be utilized when there are two distinct positions or arguments. Each group has an opportunity to discuss the issue while the other group observes. The goal of this technique is for one group to gain insight about the other perspective by having this opportunity to listen and formulate questions. After both sides have shared and listened, students are often given the opportunity to discuss their questions and ideas with students representing the other side of the argument.

A fishbowl for multiple perspectives

This format allows students to look at a question or a text from various perspectives. First, assign perspectives to groups of students. These perspectives could represent the viewpoints of different historical figures, characters in a novel, social categories (e.g., young, old, male, female, working-class laborer, industrialist, peasant, noble, soldier, priest, etc.), or political/philosophical points of view. Each group discusses the same question, event, or text representing their assigned perspective. The goal of this technique is for students to consider how perspective shapes meaning-making. After all groups have shared, students can be given the opportunity to discuss their ideas and questions with peers from other groups.

Identity Charts[1]

Rationale

Identity charts are graphic tools that help students consider the many factors that shape who we are as individuals and as communities. They can be used to deepen students' understanding of themselves, groups, nations, and historical and literary figures. Identity charts will also help students think about the identities and experiences of the young people they watch in BULLY. There are several points in this guide when it might be helpful to have students create identity charts. By comparing charts they make for themselves with those they make for people in the film, students may begin to make more explicit connections with those victimized by bullying. They may also begin to appreciate the differences that exist in their community that might make one more vulnerable to being bullied.

Procedure

Creating an identity chart for yourself

Before creating identity charts, you might have the class brainstorm categories we consider when thinking about the question, "Who am I?" such as our role in a family (e.g., daughter, sister, mother, etc.), our hobbies and interests (e.g., guitar player, football fan, etc.), our background (e.g., religion, race, nationality, hometown, or place of birth), and our physical characteristics. It is often helpful to show students a completed identity chart before they create one of their own.

Give students an opportunity to share their identity charts with one another, then follow up with a short discussion. What similarities do they notice between members of the class? What differences stand out? Are some differences more important than others? Why or why not?

Creating identity charts for people, groups, or communities in the film

First, ask students to write the name of the person, group, or community in the center of a piece of paper. Then, as students watch the film or explore readings from this guide, they can look for evidence that helps

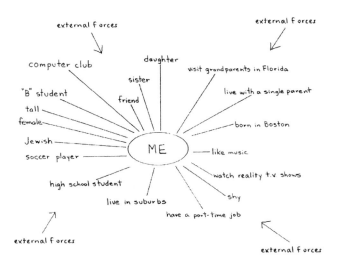

them answer the question, "Who is this person?" or "Who is this group?" Encourage students to include quotations from the film on their identity charts, as well as their own interpretations of the person or group. Students can complete identity charts individually or in small groups. Alternatively, students could contribute ideas to a class version of an identity chart that you keep on the classroom wall.

Give students an opportunity to reflect on and discuss their observations. Did they notice any similarities between themselves and the people and communities in the film? Of the characteristics they recorded for young people in the film, are there any that make them more likely to be picked on or bullied?

Variation: Identity Boxes

People have two identities: what the outside world thinks of us and an internal identity (the traits we ascribe to ourselves). To illuminate this concept, students can create identity boxes, for themselves or for people in the film. The inside of the box contains words and images that represent how we describe ourselves. The outside of the box contains words and images that represent how we think others view us.

Notes

1 Activity adapted from *Facing History and Ourselves: Holocaust and Human Behavior* (Brookline, Massachusetts: Facing History and Ourselves, 1994), 8.

Attribute Linking

Rationale

This activity is designed to help students discuss difficult issues, while also recognizing that they likely represent different perspectives. Attribute Linking can help students to define, clarify, and personalize the roles of *upstander* and *bystander*. By having students look for attributes they share before they discuss issues on which they may differ, the exercise emphasizes commonality over differences and helps students recognize the value of negotiation. Finally, this exercise builds trust and contributes to a climate of openness.

While the procedure suggested below explores the roles of upstander and bystander, this strategy may also be adapted to explore the roles of *bully* and *victim*. It is important to help students understand that *bully, victim, upstander,* and *bystander* are all roles that we each play in different situations at different times and are not fixed parts of our identities.

Procedure

1. Ask students to find someone in the room (partner #1) with their same hair color. Have these pairs of students exchange definitions of *bystander* and, if time permits, provide examples. Before proceeding, make sure each pair of students has reached a mutually agreed upon definition of *bystander* to take to their next partner.

2. Ask students to find a different person in the room (partner #2) with their same eye color. Have these new pairs share the definitions of *bystander* they each brought from their first partner. Then, have these new pairs exchange stories of incidents in their lives when they witnessed bullying and acted as a bystander. If students cannot think of an incident they witnessed, they may share one they saw on television or read about in the newspaper.

   Ask each pair to make a list of at least three reasons bystanders might choose to do nothing when they witness bullying. Have students use felt-tip markers to record these lists on colored construction paper to post around the room.

3. Ask students to find a new partner in the room (partner #3) with the same size hand. Students must measure their hands, palm-to-palm, in order to find a match. Have these pairs of students exchange definitions of *upstander* and, if time permits, provide examples. Before proceeding, make sure each pair of students has reached a mutually agreed upon definition of *upstander* to take to their next partner.

4. Ask students to find a new partner (partner #4) who is their same height. Once again, students must measure themselves by standing back-to-back with potential partners until they find a match. Have these new pairs share the definitions of *upstander* they each brought from their previous partner. Then, have students exchange stories about incidents involving bullying in which they or someone they know acted as an upstander. If students cannot think of an incident they witnessed, they may share one they saw on television or read about in the newspaper.

   Ask each pair to make a list of at least three actions upstanders might take when they witness bullying. Have students use felt-tip markers to record these lists on colored construction paper to post around the room.

5. After posting their bystander and upstander lists, have all students read through their classmates' lists and discuss them in simultaneous, informal conversations with their partners and other classmates. Once all have finished posting their definitions and had a chance to read the others', debrief the activity.

6. It is critical to debrief this activity thoroughly. The discussion should include the following points:
   - the variety of reasons bystanders do not act
   - the variety of actions an upstander might take to help
   - the fact that we "play" both roles in different situations at different times
   - the fact that we can "play" the roles of bully and victim in different situations at different times

Big Paper

Rationale

This discussion strategy uses writing and silence as tools to help students explore a topic in depth. Having a written conversation with peers slows down students' thinking process and gives them an opportunity to focus on the views of others. This strategy also creates a visual record of students' thoughts and questions that can be referred to later. Using the *Big Paper* strategy can help engage shy students who are not as likely to participate in a verbal discussion.

Procedure

1. Preparation

First, you will need to select the "stimulus"—the material that students will respond to. As the stimulus for a Big Paper activity, teachers have used questions, quotations, historical documents, and excerpts from novels, poetry, or images. For instance, if using this strategy to discuss the reading "The Power of Friendship," you might print and cut out the quotations from the film (from Kelby, Trey, and Alex and his mother) to use as the stimulus. You might also choose to use any of the Connections questions in this guide as a stimulus for this activity.

Groups can be given the same stimulus for discussion, but more often they are given different texts related to the same theme. This activity works best when students are working in pairs or triads. Make sure that all students have a pen or marker. Some teachers have students use different colored markers to make it easier to see the back-and-forth flow of a conversation. Each group also needs a "big paper" (typically a sheet of poster paper) that can fit a written conversation and added comments. In the middle of the page, tape or write the "stimulus" (image, quotation, excerpt, etc.) that will be used to spark the students' discussion.

2. The importance of silence

Inform the class that this activity will be completed in silence. All communication is done in writing. Students should be told that they will have time to speak in pairs and in large groups later. Go over all of the instructions at the beginning so that they do not ask questions during the activity. Also, before the activity starts, the teacher should ask students if they have questions, to minimize the chance that students will interrupt the silence once it has begun. You can also remind students of their task as they begin each new step.

3. Comment on your Big Paper

Each group receives a Big Paper and each student a marker or pen. The groups read the text in silence. After students read the text, they may comment on the text and ask questions of each other in writing on the Big Paper. The written conversation must start on the text but can stray to wherever the students take it. If someone in the group writes a question, another member of the group should address the question by writing on the Big Paper. Students can draw lines connecting a comment to a particular question. Make sure students know that more than one of them can write on the Big Paper at the same time. The teacher can determine the length of this step, but it should be at least 15 minutes.

4. Comment on other Big Papers

Still working in silence, the students leave their partner(s) and walk around reading the other Big Papers. Students bring their marker or pen with them and can write comments or further questions for thought on other Big Papers. Again, the teacher can determine the length of time for this step based on the number of Big Papers and his or her knowledge of the students.

5. Return to your own Big Paper

Silence is broken. The pairs rejoin back at their own Big Paper. They should look at any comments written by others. Now they can have a free, verbal conversation about the text, their own comments, what they read on other papers, and comments their fellow students wrote back to them. At this point, you might ask students to take out their journals and identify a question or comment that stands out to them at this moment.

6. Class discussion

Finally, debrief the process with the large group. The conversation can begin with a simple prompt such as, "What did you learn from doing this activity?" This is the time to delve deeper into the content and use ideas on the Big Papers to bring out students' thoughts. The discussion can also touch upon the importance and difficulty of staying silent and the level of comfort with this activity.

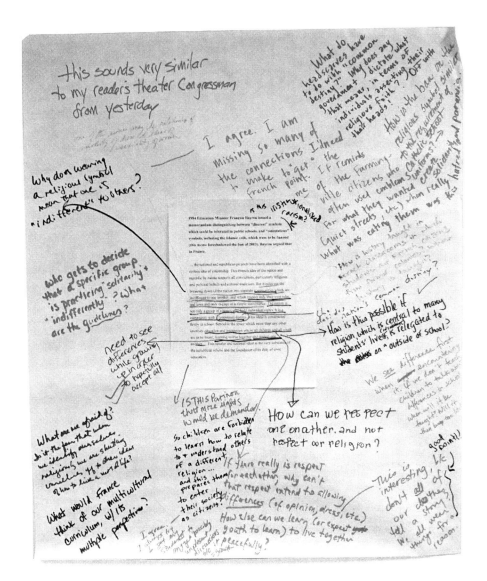

Think, Pair, Share

Rationale

This discussion technique gives students the opportunity to thoughtfully respond to questions in written form and to engage in meaningful dialogues with other students around important issues. Asking students to write and discuss ideas with a partner before sharing with the larger group gives students more time to compose their ideas. This format helps students build confidence, encourages greater participation, and often results in more thoughtful discussions. This strategy may be used to facilitate discussion around any Connections question in this guide.

Procedure

1. Think
Have students reflect on a given question or write a response in their journals.

2. Pair
Have students pair up with one other student and share their responses.

3. Share
When the larger group reconvenes, ask pairs to report back on their conversations. Alternatively, you could ask students to share what their partner said. In this way, this strategy focuses on students' skills as careful listeners.

Improving the Script

Rationale

BULLY includes a variety of exchanges between parents, school officials, and young people that many viewers will find unsatisfactory. While it is often easy to critique the responses to the bullying that young people experience in the film, it is perhaps more useful to think about what kinds of responses are most helpful and productive. In this Improving the Script activity, participants are asked to rewrite some of the dialogue from the film to reflect how they would like members of their community to respond to bullying. Consider using this activity with adults as well as students in your school community.

Procedure

1. Selecting a scene

The reading "Adult Intervention" includes short passages of dialogue between school officials and students who have been bullied. Either can be used for this activity. Alternatively, students and adults may choose any scene from the movie in which they found an adult response to bullying to be unsatisfactory and create a short dialogue from scratch to reflect how the response could be improved.

2. Writing the script

In groups of two or three, participants can discuss what they find ineffective about the adult response in the scene they chose. Then, they should discuss how they would like the adult to have responded. Finally, they can work together to construct and script a better response.

3. Sharing and debrief

After reconvening, each small group can share with the whole their improved scripts. Participants can then discuss similarities and differences that emerge in their ideas about how adults can best respond to young people's experiences of bullying.

Save the Last Word for Me

Rationale

Save the Last Word for Me is a discussion strategy that requires all students to participate as active speakers and listeners. Its clearly defined structure helps shy students share their ideas and ensures that frequent speakers practice being quiet. It is often used as a way to help students debrief a reading or film.

Procedure

1. Preparation

Identify a reading or video excerpt that will serve as the catalyst for this activity.

2. Students read and respond to text

Have students read or view the selected text. Ask students to highlight three sentences that particularly stood out for them and write each sentence on the front of an index card. On the back they should write a few sentences explaining why they chose that quote— what it meant to them, reminded them of, etc. They may have connected it to something that happened to them in their own life, to a film or book they saw or read, or to something that happened in history or is happening in current events.

3. Sharing in small groups

Divide the students into groups of three, labeling one student A, one B, and the other C. Invite the A's to read one of their chosen quotations. Students B and C then discuss the quotation while student A remains silent. What do they think it means? Why do they think these words might be important? To whom? After several minutes, ask the A students to read the backs of their cards (or to explain why they picked the quotation), thus having "the last word." This process continues with student B sharing and then student C.

CPSIA information can be obtained at www.ICGtesting.com
Printed in the USA
BVOW051542040612

291574BV00006B/1/P